Involving Physicians
in Product Line Marketing

Involving Physicians
in Product Line Marketing

*Lynne Cunningham, MPA
and Charles Koch, MA*

Pluribus Press, Inc., Chicago

© 1987 by Pluribus Press, Inc.
All Rights Reserved

Except for appropriate use in critical reviews, or works of scholarship, the reproduction or use of this work in any form or by any electronic, mechanical or other means now known or hereafter invented, including photocopying and recording, and in any information storage and retrieval system is forbidden without the permission of the publisher.

91 90 89 88 87   5 4 3 2 1

Library of Congress Catalog Number
87-60401

International Standard Book Number:
0-931028-93-0

Pluribus Press, Inc.
160 East Illinois Street
Chicago, Illinois 60611

Printed in the United States of America

To Patrick G. Hays, President and Chief Executive Officer, Sutter Health System, Sacramento, California

Contents

Introduction / 1

1 Physicians and Hospitals—A New Marketing Partnership / 7

1—Methods for Physician Interaction / 9
2—PRIMOe: A Model for Structured Involvement / 25
3—Trust Building / 57
4—Patient Research / 63
5—More Questions and More Answers / 75

2 Real World Examples / 89

1—Geriatrics, Marsha A. Vacca / 91
2—Heart Center, Steven A. Fellows / 99
3—Obstetrical Services, Karen Corrigan / 109
4—Oncology Services, Stanley B. Berry / 115
5—Trauma Care, Peter M. Dawson / 121

Index / 129

Introduction

Norfolk (Virginia) General Hospital opened its women's health pavilion late in 1986, three years after contemplating leaving obstetrical and gynecological services to other hospitals in its area. What changed the hospital's direction was research conducted by an internal product management team that uncovered both consumer needs and physician recommendations for facility and service changes that would augment an already respected program for managing complicated pregnancies. Physician input to the planning and marketing of the new program was acquired both on an informal basis and through the OB/Gyn committee of the medical staff. As the new center moved closer to operation, physicians were asked to participate more regularly in planning and marketing meetings and their involvement is expected to become more formalized in the near future.

At Sutter Community Hospitals, a unit of Sutter Health System, Sacramento, California, physicians were directly involved in developing the marketing plan for its geriatrics program through participation in a multidisciplinary task force. In particular, members of the medical staff played important roles in designing the survey instrument for research on the "older" market in the community and in reviewing the results of that study. The task force also has been responsible for developing several new programs for older adults and their families and for extending awareness of the services available at Sutter throughout the medical staff.

Maintaining and building its market share in cardiology was the problem faced by another unit of the Sutter Health System, Sutter Memorial Hospital. Because cardiovascular surgery occurs only at the end of a long line of referrals, many disciplines had to be represented on a steering committee to improve the hospitals marketing position: surgeons, adult and pediatric cardiologists, critical care nurses, primary care practitioners and administrative and operations managers. Following preliminary data gathering, the steering committee directed a formal research program to identify referring physician groups and to find out what they liked and didn't like about the Sutter program. The results of the research were discussed with the medical staff members, an educational program was undertaken, and a community public relations effort was launched.

The marketing effort that developed from these efforts and the program changes that were initiated have not been formally evaluated, but the initial results appear favorable.

An in-depth survey of physicians in its community led Sonora (California) Community Hospital to emphasize and expand its oncology services. The hospital is one of two serving an area with 40,000 residents. Thus, long-range survival depends on a strategy of providing unique or special services to the community. Previously the hospital had acted on the results of a survey of the general public to establish an urgent care program that raised visits to its emergency department by 30 per cent. Now the administration wanted to know if a coordinated oncology program was needed and would be well received by area physicians. Individual interviews with a representative group of doctors were conducted not only to verify the need but to gain support for such a program. With the oncology services now in place, the hospital expects to continue formalized interviews as a method of obtaining physician feedback and support.

Although all the acute care facilities in its area had emergency departments, Norfolk General Hospital felt there were several reasons it should market a trauma center: no competitor had staked out that territory, trauma care was an emerging product line, and such a program complemented other programs of the hospital's such as neuroscience and burn care. A trauma marketing task force representing those and other interests was formed and met at least once or twice a month to direct the development of such specific projects as formation of a trauma team and marketing ideas. Implementation was delegated to subcommittees. As a result of these efforts, the volume of trauma cases at the hospital has increased more than four times and continuing market research will attempt to spot other opportunities for development.

What do these five seemingly disparate situations have in common? They are all examples of how physician participation in product line marketing can result in a stronger, more successful hospital and offer new opportunities to the medical staff. They also point the way to survival in today's highly competitive environment.

Physician involvement in product line marketing is a necessity today for those hospitals that wish to effectively compete in a competitive health care market place. The significance of physicians and hospitals working in partnership is tantamount to the effective marketing function. A marketing process which sincerely integrates the physician as a "coprovider" may mark the difference for the viability of the organization.

Business arrangements have overshadowed the mutually comfortable and friendly co-existence of hospitals and physicians. It is not uncommon now to observe a climate of mistrust between physicians and hospitals as a result of transactions that illustrate the new reality: each entity has a business life of its own. Yet, the nature of acute hospital services and most health care services is such that the product is and remains a combined effort of the hospital and its medical staff.

Defining the Terms

Before delving into models and methods of involvement, we'll define two terms as used in this book: product line marketing and consumer.

Product line marketing is an attempt to refocus the planning, directing and controlling of hospital resources to coincide with "service packages" that frequently follow disease entities such as cardiovascular, cancer and neurological disease. Sometimes the product line may also align and overlap with clinical specialties such as pediatrics, geriatrics and OB/Gyn. If the product line is designed to satisfy a particular market segment, it will probably be distinctly different and more dynamic than the traditional hospital and medical staff departmental structures.

Consumer is a term that includes not only the general public but also physicians, government and insurers. The consumer is any potential user of the hospital's services as well as the party involved in the purchase, direction, or payment of the services.

Product line marketing as a process recognizes the changing relationship between the hospital and its public. The strategic planning of the 70's saw physicians as the key market. However, payor contracting today is rechanneling patient publics outside the control of the physician-patient relationship.

Our historical physician-hospital coprovidership has yielded a health care product too costly and complex for the public to accept and understand. It has spurred the buyer/payor revolution putting the burden of cost and complexity back on physicians and hospital providers. The choice for the consumer becomes an assessment of insurance premium costs and perceived provider acceptability. The hospital is placed in a position of establishing and continually re-establishing its distinctive image to its market and the value of its products as packaged from the buyer/payor perspective. This is the ongoing product line marketing process.

One final preliminary note. The authors are aware

that some of the situations we describe and facts we state are common knowledge to the reader. We do not intend to be patronizing. But we include these statements in order to provide a framework for the concept of product line marketing and to supply a foundation for understanding physician involvement.

1

Physicians and Hospitals—A New Marketing Partnership

At the heart of this section is the relationship of physicians and hospitals to their markets. These basic, functioning relationships have been challenged and have changed as a result of business deals between payors and providers.

The question today is not if *physicians should be involved, but* how *physicians should be involved in the marketing process of the hospital—even though the process may yield perceived and real competing services.*

METHODS FOR PHYSICIAN INTERACTION

Physician participation in the product line marketing process is key to the successful implementation of a marketing plan.

We have identified four models for preliminary and ongoing communication and relationship building with the medical staff and three models for physician involvement in the product line process.

The approaches which can be used for preliminary and ongoing communication and relationship building include: the one-on-one, team approach, formal medical staff structure, and physician advisory group methods. A hospital may choose to use one or more of these methods simultaneously. Different methods may be more appropriate for specific product lines.

COMMUNICATION MODELS

The one-on-one or individualized approach builds on informal and positive relationships between the administrator and individual physicians. This approach is invaluable throughout product line marketing, particularly at the beginning. When establishing a product line marketing task force it is important to initiate one-on-one communication with each task force member before the process begins. This can help in the selection of a specific product line marketing committee and give you an opportunity to brief each team member on the process that will be used. This one-on-one communication method should be viewed as a prelude to other models and an opportunity to build trust between you and the physician participants during the marketing process. One-on-one relationship building is essentially an opportunity for an administrator to do his or her homework and determine what hidden agendas and cards each marketing task force member will be bringing to the table. Individual sessions with each marketing task force member will allow the administrative chair of the committee to assess educational needs of committee members which can be addressed on an individual or group basis prior to committee meetings or during the group sessions. One-on-one sessions also provide an opportunity for administrative staff members to be candid about the role each physician will be playing on the marketing task force and the strategic nature of data which will be shared. This private—but candid—opportunity for discussion will also present a forum to discuss the physician's relationships with competitive facilities and the need to publicly proclaim allegiance to your facility. Even if you feel you know physician members of a marketing task force well, preliminary one-on-one sessions can help solidify your relationships, determine attitudes about various marketing components, i.e., the need for research and the use of advertising, and establish the doctor's specific role as a member of the work group.

The team approach is particularly effective if a large number of physicians are required to complete product line marketing objectives. Essentially, this is an organized approach to one-on-one sessions. This model can be used for preliminary strategy development as well as forming the foundation for ongoing maintenance of physician trust, building relationships. The team approach is a coordinated attempt by the facility's management team to assess the needs of medical staff members, obtain their input for research and planning purposes, identify educational objectives, and provide feedback. Although the process may be separate, it needs to reinforce product line marketing objectives. The team approach cannot be successful unless responsibility for coordination of all information gathered by the various members of the management team is in place.

The formal medical staff structure can be used to introduce concepts, reinforce techniques, and communicate actions. It should not be used for marketing decision making purposes. Although the main purposes of the medical staff are to carry out the bylaws, make credentialing and privileging recommendations, and implement a quality assurance program, the importance of the structure should not be overlooked during the product line marketing process. The pre-established meetings of the medical staff can be used as a forum for status reports on service changes and objective achievements related to marketing plans. This is an opportunity for physician members of a marketing task force to have some increased visibility and reinforce the active involvement of the physicians in the marketing process. The educational forum may also help in identifying additional physicians who can be involved in the marketing process in the future and are sympathetic to a comprehensive marketing approach, believing that marketing is something in addition to paid advertising.

While the organized and formal medical staff structure is at one end of a continuum, the physician advisory group is at the other end. Instead of representing the various clinical sections of the medical staff, the physician advisory group is representative of the business sectors of the hospital's staff. Most hospitals involved in product line marketing have medical staffs dominated by a variety of large single or multispecialty physician groups. It is these groups that should be represented on the physician marketing advisory group. These physicians understand they are competitors, but in the physician advisory group forum it is possible for the hospital to report on product line activities and obtain input from these competitors in an organized fashion. Participants in a physician advisory group should be hand picked by the administrative staff. The objective or goal of this group should be to develop and build trust relationships between the hospital and its major physician providers. The group should discuss general hospital business issues that relate to the overall image and business plan of the institution. This type of group should meet on an ongoing and quarterly basis.

Determining Suitability

Although the method of communication and relationship building will vary depending on the hospital, its individual situation, and medical staff politics, some generalizations can be made on situations where each of these approaches is particularly appropriate.

The one-on-one approach should be used to assess the attitudes of each physician who will participate on a new marketing task force. To provide consistency in information gathering and feedback all contact should be made by the single administrative representative who will be chairing the task force. Since the number of physicians involved will likely be small, this is a reasonable approach.

The team approach should be used on an ongoing basis to solicit input from the medical staff on general topics, the impact of new programs and services at your facility and elsewhere in the community, and the effect new laws and regulations are having on the medical staff. A senior administrative staff member should have responsibility for coordinating responses, reporting trends and, initially, identifying the subjects which will be discussed. Each member of the hospital's administrative staff should have a list of his or her "doctors" who are contacted on a regular basis. This is also an appropriate forum for sharing utilization data and determining why a physician's practice patterns are increasing or decreasing at your particular facility.

The formal medical staff structure can be used to review trends or plans that are to be implemented. For example, at a cardiology or internal medicine section meeting you might want to review a cath lab proposal or plans to expand into coronary angioplasty or laser therapy as part of the implementation of a cardiac product line marketing plan.

The physician advisory group invites discussion of the impact of alternative delivery systems on the hospital and on the groups' practices. It is the forum to discuss business system problems, implementing contracting provisions, or to evaluate the impact another teaching program will have on patient care at the facility.

PARTICIPATION MODELS

The three models for physician involvement are referred to as the medical director approach, the physician task force, and the multidisciplinary task force.

The medical director model recognizes a hospital's designated medical leader in a specialty or subspecialty. This person provides leadership and advice in a component area of a product line. This model may be the appropriate one to use for a variety of reasons.

You first need to ask who is the target audience. If the primary target audience for your product line is the physician group itself, it may be appropriate to work with a designated physician leader who can directly interface with the physician audience. This is the "intensivist" model and one that may be appropriate during the development of a critical care product line.

Perhaps the strategic nature of the development of your product line requires keeping the number of parties participating at a minimum. This is another reason to use the medical director model. By establishing a small marketing task force of hospital representatives, including a single physician, the strategic nature of your work is more likely to be preserved.

Another reason to consider the medical director model is the timing of the development of your marketing plan. Working with a single physician, particularly if this doctor is an administrative medical director who already has administrative time devoted to the facility, insures the most rapid development of a product line marketing plan while still insuring physician involvement. This may be appropriate if two competitive hospitals are racing to offer a new product or an augmentation to an existing product or if a competitor has announced the initiation of a product which has been one of your hospital's traditional strengths. Developing and implementing a product line marketing plan quickly can help preserve your existing market share.

In selecting the physician who should work with your marketing task force in the medical director model first look to any medical directors you are paying already. If there is an administrative component to their contracts, it is reasonable to expect them to be involved in this type of market planning function. You can be reasonably assured of their allegiance to your hospital if they already are serving in paid medical director roles but, as will be discussed later, this may be a drawback as well.

The physician task force model formally integrates physicians when a task requires completion. Using this model, an eight to twelve member physician task force guides the development of the product line marketing plan with staffing support from administration, marketing, and department managers. Physicians represent various specialties and sub-specialties which will be affected by the marketing plan.

For example, in the development of a marketing plan for a heart center, cardiovascular surgeons, in-house cardiologists, as well as external cardiologists and internists, might all be included on the same task force. Staff support would be provided by an assistant administrator, marketing director or marketing consultant, CCU nursing supervisor, and cardiology clinic manager. In these settings, don't overlook the role of the primary care physicians even if they are not heavy users. Assessment of referral relationships should identify the potential for primary care physician involvement.

The physician marketing task force is focused on a

single product line. For the physician task force to be successful, the administrative coordinator must understand the various levels of physician referral—from primary care physicians referring to diagnostic specialists and they in turn referring to therapeutic members of the medical staff. Because the physician task force will likely bring together different sub-specialists from diverse medical groups, it is vital that input for the process is received from everyone. Although the physician task force is a good model when a diverse group of doctors need to be educated about the marketing process, it is important to remember that this is perhaps the most time-consuming model to use and the facility must have time to nurture the task force while developing the product line marketing plan.

The multi-disciplinary task force uses a smaller number of physicians. Here a larger group of department managers and functional specialists participate freely as team members as the product line marketing plan is developed. Staff support for the multi-disciplinary task force is provided by the marketing director or marketing consultant and the administrative coordinator for the particular product line. The multi-disciplinary task force is a particularly appropriate model to use when there is a multiplicity of buyers for the product line. This will be true of diversified product lines that offer services along a broad spectrum of the health care continuum. Oncology programs, geriatric programs and obstetrics programs are good examples.

Frequently oncology programs are already organized as a team with physicians and hospital representatives participating in regular group sessions. Primary care specialty and subspecialty physicians are involved. The hospital's product line may include a clinical component and inpatient care as well as home health and hospice care. Frequently, educational programs are offered which can be selected directly by the patient and the patient's family. This product line also has considerable fund raising potential thus involving another component of the hospital family.

Geriatrics programs often are similarly organized, particularly in facilities which have a high percentage of older patients in many of their product lines. Geriatrics becomes a product line that crosses other clinical areas and essentially becomes a specialty without walls. It may also include educational programs, community outreach and in some hospitals financing mechanisms.

Obstetrics is another example of a product line which includes both inpatient physician directed components as well as outpatient and educational programs which are selected by the patient or the consumer.

The multidisciplinary task force approach is ideal to use when the product line is already set up along a team model. The multidisciplinary team may help you look at innovative ways to organize the product line, particularly if you are bringing together people who traditionally have not had regular interaction.

For example, at Sharp Memorial Hospital in San Diego, multidisciplinary marketing task forces are proposing separating the educational and research components from patient care to allow fund raising and contracting to complement each other in raising necessary resources.

How to choose

How then does the hospital decide which model will work most successfully for a particular product line. The first area to address in deciding which model will work best in a particular instance is to determine the urgency of the outcome of your product line marketing process. Do you have unique opportunities or unique threats being presented because of competitive hospitals or alternative delivery systems' entry into the market place? If there is a great deal of urgency in completing the development of a product line marketing plan, you may opt for the medical director approach to planning since this requires the least physician involvement and therefore coordination. It can be facilitated most quickly.

Next, honestly assess the breadth of ownership from the physicians participating in a particular center of excellence. Physicians can be categorized as patient brokers, coproviders and competitors.

A patient broker or independent contractor makes decisions on behalf of his or her patients and practices primarily at one institution, although the doctor may have admitting privileges at another facility.

The coprovider has traditionally been the hospital based physician. But today this category also includes physicians who are technologically aligned with the facility due to the nature of their practice. These would include cardiovascular surgeons, oncology subspecialists, neonatologists and other supersubspecialists.

The competitor has divided institutional allegiance. Additionally, his or her practice may compete with the hospital. Ophthalmologists and other surgeons with surgical capabilities in their own offices are examples. The physician owners of free-standing surgery centers, physician partners in imaging centers or free-standing cath labs are other examples.

Obviously today many physicians are fitting into more than one group. In spite of this crossover, characterizing physicians involved in a center of excellence as predominantly patient brokers, coproviders or competitors will assist greatly in determining whether or not it is appropriate to use the medical director, physician task force or multidisciplinary task force approach to physician involvement in product line marketing.

If your physicians are predominantly coproviders, the physician task force or multidisciplinary task force will be more successful. If the group is mostly competitors, the medical director approach may be the only feasible response.

It is the role of the administrative staff representative to identify which hat a physician is wearing in a particular situation. The administrator then must clarify these different roles, working with a physician, so both the administrator and the doctor are aware of the physician's particular role in any situation.

The next area to consider when identifying the correct physician involvement model to use, is the perception the medical staff will have of the quality of your product line marketing plan based on the involvement of particular individuals. This is perhaps the toughest political question you must answer, and it must be answered honestly. If the medical director of a center of excellence is well respected clinically but not necessarily administratively, it may point to the need for involvement of more physicians in the marketing process. However, if the medical director is perceived to have a pulse on all factions participating in the center of excellence, the medical director approach may facilitate the completion of the plan.

Next, you need to ask yourself how open you are to physician input in the marketing process. If you truly desire input, you may want to select the physician task force or multidisciplinary task force approaches. If you're not prepared to respond to broad based physician input, the medical director approach may be more appropriate.

The political realities of your particular institution

may also impact on your decision to use or not use the medical director approach or one of the task force approaches to product line marketing. To determine how willing you are to hear from physicians, you should ask yourself the following questions:

- What clout does your medical staff have directly with your board of trustees?
- What authority does your management staff have to implement the recommendations which will come out of the marketing process?
- What is the relationship between the management/administrative staff and the medical staff?
- What is the medical staff's knowledge of the marketing process?
- How much time will you need to spend educating the staff about marketing as you go along?
- Do the doctors understand that marketing is a process and not just another term for advertising and promotion?

Your honest answers to these questions and the political realities behind them can help you select the appropriate physician involvement.

Finally, assess the interrelationships your product line subspecialty physicians have and how referrals work among their different groups.

Your honest appraisal of this situation will help you decide how many physicians should be on a physician task force or a multidisciplinary task force. That will insure against overlooking a group that then does not buy into the results of the final plan because it was ignored.

How can you get physician support for product line marketing?

Involve them in the process! Employees and physicians will be more supportive of the final product if they have been involved in its design. There are two important times to involve physicians in the product line marketing process: During the research phase and throughout the planning process. Specific models for involvement of physicians in the research phase will be discussed in the next chapter.

If the product line market planning process is viewed as an hourglass, all physicians can be involved at the top in the broad scale research process. As you come closer to the cross section of the hourglass, which is the strategic decision point, fewer and fewer physicians are involved. But once strategic decisions are made and the facility is ready to proceed with implementation, all physicians should be involved in the communication process. The established medical staff committee structure can be used to carry the accepted information.

SOME QUESTIONS AND ANSWERS*

How do I get started involving my physicians in product line marketing?

The first step is for the administrator responsible for the center of excellence, the marketing director or marketing consultant, and the medical director of the product line to sit down and candidly perform a SWOT analysis (strengths, weaknesses, opportunities and threats) of the product line. Then they should discuss the structure

---

*Participants in the questions and answer sections following chapters 1 and 2 include: Peter Dawson, President, First Step, Norfolk, Virginia; Dana Ellerbe, Executive Director, Baylor Institute for Rehabilitation, Dallas, Texas; John Glassman, Vice President of Marketing, Stormont-Vail Regional Medical Center, Topeka, Kansas; Bill Murray, President, St. Vincent Hospital and Medical Center, Billings, Montana; and Paul Teslow, President, Health West Foundation, Chatsworth, California.

of a marketing task force and physician involvement in the research and planning process.

Decide if physicians other than the medical director should be involved in the planning process and if staff members other than physicians should be involved.

Before the first meeting of the marketing task force is held, however, it is important for the administrator and/or marketing director to meet with every person who will be on the task force to determine their level of knowledge about marketing, (i.e. is marketing an exchange process balancing needs with programs and services or is marketing "just advertising?") The first meeting or meetings of the marketing task force should be devoted to an overview of the marketing process or marketing model which will be used, the need for product line marketing, the physician's role in the process, and a SWOT analysis of the product line from the perspective of the marketing task force.

Once these initial steps are taken, research can be planned and implemented and the marketing task force can provide feedback on research results and implications for the product line. The more involvement the marketing task force and the physicians on that task force have during the planning stage, the more likely they will be supportive of the product line marketing plan.

How can we get physicians to support product line marketing?

As you are gathering information about the clinical product line and the perceived needs of the physicians and their patients, involve as many physicians as possible in the research process. This can be done through individual interviews, physician focus groups or integrated focus groups.

Individual interviews are the best research method to use if only a limited number of physicians must be contacted or if their conflicting schedules would make it difficult to conduct a focus group, e.g., emergency physicians. Using a prescribed interview guideline, the physician's opinion about the strengths, weaknesses, opportunities and threats (SWOT) faced by the product line are solicited.

Segregated physician focus groups can be successfully used when a large number of physicians should participate in the research process and the doctors have more flexible schedules. Focus groups can be organized by subspecialty or clinical emphasis. The team model presupposes who on the management team could best interrelate with which physicians and on what planning issues. The degree of formalization should coincide with the number of physicians needed for "buy in" as based on anticipated medical staff barriers.

The medical director approach to product line market planning involves the participation of the product line medical director on an administrative marketing task force. This is a model to use when the marketing plan must be completed rapidly because of strategic or competitive forces or when a large number of the physicians involved in the product line are viewed as competitors rather than coproviders.

The physician marketing task force is a model to use when a large number of physician subspecialists must be involved in the market planning process—and the focus is on *process*. For example, in developing a heart product line marketing plan, it may be necessary to involve adult cardiovascular surgeons, adult in-house cardiologists, adult external cardiologists, pediatric cardiologists, pediatric cardiovascular surgeons, etc. If competitive forces do not necessitate the quick turn around of a product line marketing plan, it may be important to take six months or more to develop the plan and ensure that all physicians have an opportunity to actively participate in the plan's development and communicate with their respective colleagues.

On the other hand, if the product line is already organized using a multidisciplinary approach, it may make more sense to have an integrated marketing task force with physicians, nurses and ancillary personnel participating on an equal basis. This approach, obviously, creates a team spirit for marketing and ensures that all players in a process have an equal opportunity to have input into the plan.

PRIMOe: A Model for Structured Involvement

Whether a hospital is large or small, is dealing with a facility-wide marketing plan or a plan for a specific product line, we have found there are consistent needs when it comes to marketing:

- There is a need to educate a large number of people about the marketing process and instill in them an understanding that marketing is more than the advertising component of promotion.

- If marketing plans are to be developed for a variety of product lines in the same facility, there is a need for a simple marketing model. If all product line managers are trained in the use of the same model, initial plans can be developed and annual marketing plans can be updated more easily. This also facilitates the research and budgeting process for the entire hospital if needs are identified in a consistent manner. When a marketing model is simple to use and all department heads are trained to develop plans using its steps, everyone can more easily be involved in market plan development than if the model is complex and can only be developed by a trained marketing professional.

A single model for market plan development facilitates the structured involvement of the hospital's management, department heads, and staff. Hospitals that consistently use a marketing task force approach to the development of product line marketing plans will find department heads, physicians and employees readier to accept the implementation of new programs and changes or augmentations to existing programs. When this same type of involvement is expected from management and hospital staff whenever a product line marketing plan is developed, they have a better understanding of what their roles will be and how they interface with marketing professionals.

- Finally, hospitals have the need for a simplified marketing model that will facilitate the effective integration of physicians throughout the market planning process. The structured involvement of physicians can assist them in learning more about marketing while they are applying marketing principles to the development of a planning document for a specific product line. Again, if physicians become accustomed to a certain level of participation in the market planning process and see their colleagues benefitting from this type of experience, they are more likely to actively participate in research and planning activities surrounding their own center of excellence or product line.

In response to these needs, the PRIMOe model (Purpose, Research and Analysis, Internal Audience, Marketing Mix, Objective Setting and evaluation) of market based planning was developed. The PRIMOe model has been used in developing facility-wide marketing plans, product line plans and department specific marketing plans. It is flexible enough to be used by seasoned marketing professionals, hospital department heads or volunteers. It is simple enough that it can be adapted to the market planning needs of an entire facility, a product line, a department or a new program or service. PRIMOe's evolving steps facilitate the education process, so important for newcomers to marketing, and ensure analysis of the marketing purpose and the proper design of the product before looking at promotional opportunities including advertising.

In developing a product line marketing plan, encourage executives, nursing staff, department managers and physicians of the affected product line to participate. If you involve key individuals in strategy development, you ensure successful strategy implementation.

In describing the PRIMOe model, we will explore its adaptability in developing product line or center of excellence marketing plans for obstetrics, cancer and heart disease.

P = PURPOSE

The first step in designing a successful product line marketing plan is to determine a specific purpose or market-

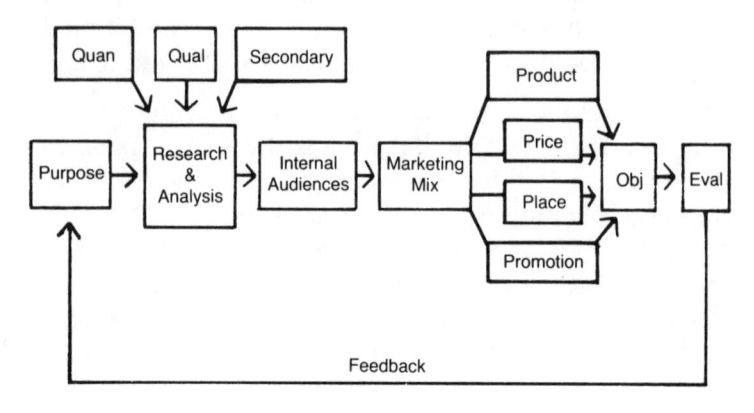

```
    Quan    Qual   Secondary           Product
      ↓      ↓      ↓                    ↓
                                       Price
              Research    Internal   Marketing          
  Purpose →     &     →   Audiences →   Mix    →          → Obj → Eval
              Analysis                         Place
     ↑                                       Promotion
     |                                          
     └─────────────────── Feedback ──────────────────────┘
```

PRIMOe Model

ing mission for the product line. Although the marketing purpose may not be finalized until research and analysis steps have been completed, it is important to develop a draft marketing mission statement to guide the development of the rest of the marketing plan. Although there are variations in the purpose statement, the marketing mission of a product line usually will fall into one of three broad categories:

- Provide a community service.

- Offer a comprehensive service package for contracting purposes or engender patient loyalty for additional programs.

- Increase market share or value to:

—provide a positive financial contribution to the hospital.
—achieve a volume level that can have an impact on quality of care.

For example, the purpose of marketing an obstetrical center of excellence might be:

- Capture patient loyalty during a first hospital experience.
- Provide a comprehensive service package for contracting purposes.
- Engender the loyalty of OB/Gyn specialists who have moved their Gyn surgeries to another hospital because your facility did not offer obstetrical services.

Although hospital obstetrical programs can make a positive financial contribution to the hospital's bottom line, many do not. They should assess the impact a positive obstetrical experience can have on future loyalty to the facility.

The oncology and heart center product lines will likely contribute positively to the hospital's bottom line. Their marketing purpose is at least partly financial: To make money.

Many heart centers will ascribe a regional mission to their centers of excellence and begin looking at super subspecialty services such as pediatric open heart surgery, heart transplants and the use of the artificial heart.

An oncology center is more likely to have a primary mission that involves supporting patients in their own community. The hospital may, in turn, develop a network which supports tertiary needs of cancer patients.

The development of the marketing mission statement or purpose statement, even in draft form, should be done by the facility's management representatives before determining which methods for physician interaction in the market planning process are most appropriate. Once a marketing mission direction has been established, the marketing director and administrative representative for the product line can engage in one-on-one interviews with key physician leaders and medical directors to determine which approaches for further physician involvement in the product line marketing process will work most effectively.

In some hospitals, department managers and physicians do not have any trouble comprehending the importance of formalizing a mission statement that speaks to the hospital's financial goals and directions for a specific product line. In other facilities, department managers and physicians alike will have major concerns about this focus on the financial aspects of marketing. They will insist that, "If we provide a high quality service, of course we will have patients." In a competitive era, there are typically several facilities offering the same product line with a similar level of perceived quality. Differentiation comes in specific product features, the comprehensiveness of the product line and the way in which the program is communicated.

As Trout and Reis so eloquently point out in their popular book, *Positioning: The Battle for Your Mind*, quality is the weakest positioning strategy that can be developed for a service as it is the easiest to erode. When the general consumer assumes that medical quality at two facilities is the same, one can begin attracting patients by focusing promotion on attributes which the consumer has the ability to measure: Lower cost, greater convenience, gourmet food or chauffered limousine rides home following surgery.

The appropriate time to look at the purpose or marketing mission of the product line is before further steps in the process have occurred. Even if this analysis only proceeds to the point of determining whether the service should make money, should be financed from philanthropic contributions or solely contribute to the hospital's ability to offer a comprehensive contracting package, the discussion of the marketing purpose of the product line is a vital step if the plan is to be successfully implemented.

R = RESEARCH AND ANALYSIS

Research and analysis are basic to developing the marketing mix and implementing cost effective strategies. Before looking specifically at physician involvement in the research process, let's consider the segmentation of target markets for research purposes.

Working with the marketing task force, which, as has been discussed previously, includes at least some physicians, brainstorm all potential target markets that may be impacted by the product line marketing plan. This means segmenting the community consumer audience by age, sex, disease entity, geographic area of residence, income level, etc. It is important that target markets do not just include patients, but also their families, the general community, support agencies, funding agencies, employers, HMOs, PPOs and the media. The PRIMOe model includes a specific reminder about internal audiences, but they should be incorporated in the potential target markets that are brainstormed at this point.

The physician target audiences for research purposes can be subdivided into specialists and subspecialists working in the product line, referring physicians who are not on your staff, primary care referring physicians who are on your staff, coproviders who impact the product line and competitors. You should also carefully consider which employees will impact on the successful marketing of the product line. These will likely include not only nursing employees working in the specific product line, but also ancillary and support personnel who have daily contact with your patients as well as business, service and other support personnel who may only see the patient at the beginning or end of the stay.

Let's take a look at how this segmentation can be applied to our three product lines.

With the obstetrical product line, women who have had children should be segmented from those who have never had children. New community residents, high risk women and women over thirty years of age will also be separate target markets. On the physicians' side, OB/Gyn specialists active on your staff should be segmented from those in the area who are not active on your staff, from family practitioners who do some obstetrics, and from family practitioners who refer patients with obstetrical or gynecological surgical needs. Many hospitals look at the obstetrical product line as a maternal and child health service and, therefore, would also segment pediatricians and neonatologists separately for research purposes.

With the oncology center of excellence, family and friends of cancer patients take on increased importance. They view this area as very "high touch." Other target audiences for the oncology product line may include community support services, funding agencies, employers interested in work site cancer prevention education, and community members interested in educational programs. Physician segments for the oncology product line would include medical, surgical and radiation oncologists, primary care physicians who refer to these specialists, subspecialty oncology physicians who are coproviders with the hospital, and oncologists who are competitors with the hospital because they provide outpatient chemotherapy services in their own offices. Depending on the nature of the cancer center, your physician target audiences may include physicians on your own staff, other physicians in the community and physicians in a broad regional area who may refer to the center of excellence.

Some consumers want high tech as well as high touch services and the heart product line is a good example. Target markets for a cardiac center of excellence might include people with a history of heart disease, smokers, those who are overweight, and members of the American Heart Association. Past patients and family members of heart patients should also be considered when looking at potential target markets. Physicians, obviously, include cardiologists and cardiovascular surgeons, but in most communities, these groups will be further subdivided. Cardiologists likely include hospital based coprovider cardiologists as well as external pediatric and adult cardiologists who, in some cases, may be competitors with the hospital, especially if they own or are partners in their own freestanding cardiac catheterization laboratory. With the heart product line, as with the oncology service, it is important to also segment family practitioners, specialists and generalists in the community but not on your hospital staff, and physicians in your referral area when developing a research plan.

Once the brainstorming of potential target markets has been considered in concert with the marketing task force, allow this group the opportunity to explore known facts about each target market and identify necessary data which should be identified during the research process. This list of "know" and "need to know" then forms the basis of survey questionnaires and focus group outlines. Research then, essentially, becomes a matter of validating what is already known and uncovering what needs to be known about each potential target audience. As it is determined what is known and needs to be known about each audience, certain similarities will be seen among many of the target audiences. This then will allow for consolidation and conservation of the research dollar.

Since it is not the purpose of this book to provide a comprehensive discussion of how product line research can be conducted, our discussion will be limited to physicians who have been identified as potential target audiences.

Regardless of the model selected for physician involvement in the actual product line marketing process—medical director, physician task force or multidisciplinary task force—the opinions of the medical staff should be solicited during the research phases of planning. There are three models which can be used for obtaining this physician input: Individual interviews, segregated physician focus groups, and multidisciplinary focus groups.

Individual interviews can be used to solicit opinions of targeted physicians when the attitude of the group is apt to be counterproductive to your desired outcomes.

Using the *segregated physician format*, focus groups made up solely of physicians are organized. The physicians may represent a variety of subspecialties within the center of excellence or may be further segregated by subspecialty.

Using the *multidisciplinary focus group* approach, physicians, nurses and ancillary personnel are segregated by subspecialty within the center of excellence and their opinions are solicited.

Whichever research methodology is selected, a specific individual interview/focus group question outline should be developed and used by the researchers conducting the study. This will ensure consistency in the information gathered and enable the researchers to weigh the responses.

To determine which model for physician research to use, consider the following questions:

- What is the style in which the product line or center of excellence is currently organized? If it is organized by internal disciplines, a multidisciplinary task force is probably appropriate. If it is organized by medical specialties or subspecialties, the segregated task forces are more appropriate. If there is no organization, you should probably use individual interviews.

- What is the style of the administrator or marketing director who will be facilitating the process? The answer to this question, which must be candid, relates directly to the degree of responsiveness and the relationships which were explored when deciding which model for physician involvement in the planning process should be used.

- If the facility is using a consultant for market planning processes, how can research be conducted most cost effectively? Depending on existing relationships with the medical staff and their sensitivity toward development of the product line marketing plan, it may be necessary for an impartial third-party consultant to conduct all research. However, if the marketing plan is being developed to strengthen an existing successful program rather than to rejuvenate a deteriorating service and good relationships exist between administration and the medical staff, it may be possible for internal resources to conduct at least some of the physician research.

- Is a fall-back position needed? If you decide to conduct focus groups and nobody comes, how long will it take to set up individual interviews, and will physicians be more likely to participate?

After you have considered the various target audience segments in which your physicians should be divided, be sure to spend some time considering the importance of each doctor's own office staff. Research can be conducted quite inexpensively with this group either by phone or mail. Office staff personnel are typically "thrilled" to be included in the research process and can become tremendous allies as you begin the implementation of the product line marketing plan.

Let's look at our three product line examples again. In developing an obstetrical service product line marketing plan, it may be necessary to focus on individual interviews and do a limited number of focus groups. Frequently, OB product line marketing plans are developed in a highly competitive atmosphere and the less open discussion of the market planning process that occurs, the better. Physician focus groups for an OB product line could probably be done with staff obstetricians segregated from staff family practitioners who do some obstetrics. Individual interviews should be conducted with physicians who the hospital would like to see increase their activity at the facility and with physicians who are among the highest admitters to the service. It is usually a good idea to do individual interviews with the highest and lowest admitters to a service and reserve focus groups for "middle admitters."

With the heart product line, physician focus groups could be conducted with doctors involved in the diagnostic process separated from doctors involved in surgery and treatment. For most heart centers, it probably will be necessary to conduct individual, in-person or telephone interviews with physicians in a regional referral area.

Frequently, oncology product lines are already organized with a multidisciplinary team approach. This is when the multidisciplinary focus group is most appropriate. Different focus groups can look at research, education, diagnostics and therapeutics, but focus group participants in each will include physicians, nursing staff and ancillary support personnel.

The primary research which should be incorporated into the development of a product line marketing plan should also include a competition analysis. Some competition is obvious and will be apparent to any marketing task force—the hospital down the street with a similar service or the regional medical center in the next town with a competing service. However, the marketing task force must carefully analyze less traditional forms of competition. These may include physician owned and operated free-standing birthing centers, home deliveries assisted by a midwife, spas and health clubs which offer special exercise programs for pregnant women, and independent contractors who offer childbirth education classes. In the oncology product line, many physicians offer outpatient chemotherapy services in their own offices and some family practitioners are reluctant to refer to oncology specialists for fear of losing their patients. The American Cancer Society may be a competitor for educational programs or fund raising resources. The heart product line needs to consider the competitive impact of physician office-based or physician-owned—but free-standing—diagnostic and rehabilitation services as well as health clubs which offer physician supervised exercise programs for patients with heart problems. Again the American Heart Association may be a competitor for education and philanthropic resources.

All of these product lines may also have internal competitors at your hospital. Do Lamaze classes at an OB clinic sponsored by the hospital compete for participants with classes sponsored by the hospital Education Department? Is the hospital a partner in a free standing cath lab which competes with your hospital based service or does one hospital in your system compete with another for the same patients?

Most hospitals also have a wealth of secondary research information available to participants in the marketing planning process. This information is typically available from the state office of health planning, the health systems agency, the state hospital association, or a regional hospital conference. It may include discharge studies, patient origin studies, and cost information. Data available from other government sources, including the Census Bureau, will help you determine demographic characteristics of your service area population. For example, how many women between 15 and 34 years of age live in your area now and what is the projected population of this age group five and 10 years from now? What are the fertility rates in the area and how have these been changing? Tumor registries can assist in identifying cancer incidence rates for your area, region or the state. Data collected by the professional review organization (PRO) in your area can be used to determine activity of various hospitals in specific major diagnostic categories (MDC). Although much of this data is 12 to 18 months old before it is publicly available, it still can help identify the scope of activities of hospital competitors, assist in determining where outmigration of patients is occurring and enable you to see how your costs compare to similar hospitals.

A final thought on research—it does not have to be expensive. The best way to gather research data on an ongoing basis is a concept borrowed from Tom Peters—research by wandering around (RBWA). If you have identified the types of information that you need on an ongoing basis, and "think research" every time you are doing rounds or following Peter's management by wandering around example, you should be successful in monitoring the pulse of your organization. Of course, research by wandering around should not be a substitute for initial base line research and research conducted formally on a periodic basis but it can help you organize your thoughts and discussions particularly with members of your medical staff when you are conducting other hospital activities.

I = INTERNAL AUDIENCE

Although the discussion of potential target markets is typically directed to external audiences, we already have discussed the importance of including physician market segments and employee market segments when we brainstormed our list of potential target audiences. The PRIMOe model forces the marketing task force to look at these internal audiences which will have a major impact on marketing a product line.

This segment of the model is also our reminder to you that internal audiences—your physicians and employees—are your most important marketing resources. We call this "Think Strawberries" after a story told by James Lavenson who took over the Plaza Hotel in New York.

When Lavenson became President of the Plaza he was no newcomer to the hotel. For ten years he had his office in a little building next door to the Plaza and went to the hotel every day for lunch and often stayed overnight. In short, he was a professional guest and everyone knows that no one knows more about how to run a hotel than a guest.

"Frankly I think the hotel business has been one of the most backward in the world," notes Lavenson.

"There's been very little change in the attitude of room clerks in the 2,000 years since Joseph arrived in Bethlehem and was told they had lost his reservation."

Lavenson felt that hotel salesmanship was retailing at its worst and started a program designed to make the Plaza's 1,400 employees into genuine hosts or hostesses. When Lavenson first came to the hotel and would ask the difference between an $85 suite and a $125 suite the reservationist proudly proclaimed "$40!" When the bell captain was asked "What's going on in the Persian Room tonight?" his answer would be "Some singer."

Dr. Ernest Dichter, head of the Institute of Motivational Research, talks about restaurant service. He has reached a classic conclusion: when people come to a fine restaurant they are hungrier for recognition than they are for food. Lavenson believes it's true. "If the maitre d' says 'We have your table ready Mr. Lavenson,' then as far as I'm concerned the chef can burn the steak and I'll be happy."

Once Lavenson's 1,400 employees were labeled and smiling he turned them into a real sales force. Today it is in the contract of every Persian Room entertainer that he or she first performs for the Plaza employees in the cafeteria before opening in the Persian Room. The movies shown on the hotel room TVs are running continuously in the employee cafeteria and new room clerks spend the night in the hotel and tour the 1,000 guest rooms as part of their orientation.

At the Plaza, the new secret oath was "everybody sells" and Lavenson meant everybody—maids, cashiers, waiters, bellman, the works. He talked to the maids about suggesting room service. To the doorman about mentioning dinner in the Plaza's restaurant. To cashiers about suggesting return reservations to departing guests and to waiters about strawberries.

Lavenson's suggestions for selling strawberries fell

on responsive ears when he described a part of the "everybody sells" program for the Oyster Bar restaurant. He figured with the same number of customers in the Oyster Bar that if the waiters would ask every customer if he'd like a second drink, wine or beer with the meal and then dessert, given only one out of four takers they'd increase sales volumes by $364,000 a year. The waiters were way ahead of the lecture—they'd already figured out that was another $50,000 in tips.

While the waiters appreciated this automatic raise in theory they were quick to point out the traditional negatives: "Nobody eats dessert anymore. Everyone's on a diet. If we served our chocolate cheesecake to everyone in the restaurant half of them would be dead in a week."

"So we'll sell them strawberries!" said Lavenson and introduced the dessert cart. They widened the aisles between the tables and had the waiter wheel the cart to each and every table at dessert time. Not daunted by the diet protestations of the customer, the waiter then went into raptures about the bowl of fresh strawberries flown in that morning from California and one out of two customers ordered them. Then Lavenson began a weekly program of showing the waiters what's happening to strawberry sales. "This month they have doubled again, so have second martinis and believe me when you get a customer for a second martini you've got a sitting duck for strawberries—with whipped cream."

"Think strawberries" became the Plaza's new secret weapon. As can be seen from Lavenson's example, no amount of money spent on product features or slick advertising campaigns can be as productive as positive communications initiated by physicians and employees directly involved with your product line.

Department or medical staff meetings can be used to communicate the status of the market planning process. However, as was pointed out earlier, be sure that the discussion is relevant and appropriate to a specific section. To gain support and input from other internal audiences, management and non-management staff, be sure to keep them informed as well through normal communication channels.

M = MARKETING MIX

Product, place, price and promotion are the next considerations. Using the information gleaned in the research and analysis phase, decide what the product should look like to meet the needs identified by your various target audiences. Obviously, as you begin costing out the expenses associated with various product components and the likelihood that a particular target audience will buy the product, you may decide to eliminate some potential target audiences or some specialized product features.

Once you have developed an initial product description, you should again turn to the research data to identify a positioning strategy for each target market. The positioning strategy is essentially an attempt to describe the product in terms each target audience wants to hear. Although the product will be the same, the way it is positioned for each of the target audiences may be different.

For example, in an obstetrical center of excellence, the patient might want the product positioned as a service that provides maximum involvement of the patient and her spouse. The physician, on the other hand, might be more interested in the availability of anesthesia and convenient parking. The product then would be marketed to the couple planning to have a child as one which is family centered where the couple designs the experience they want to have. On the other hand, the product would be marketed to the physicians by focusing on the availability of 24 hour OB anesthesia and convenient reserved parking for the obstetrician.

The cancer center should be typically positioned to the patient as "high touch" care designed to alleviate pain. The subspecialty oncology surgeon, however, wants the product line positioned as "high tech" and would like to see the focus on his/her opportunities for publishing research findings.

In the heart center product line, the cardiac rehabilitation program would be positioned as a product that allows the patient to return to work or other activities quickly. However, the center would be positioned to cardiovascular surgeons by stressing block scheduling of operating room time and the quality of nursing staff in the coronary care unit.

The importance of developing a target audience-specific positioning strategy or statement becomes a crucial link as the place, price and promotional aspects of the marketing mix are explored.

Traditionally, hospital services have been delivered in an inpatient acute setting. The place then was easy to identify. Today, executives must work to creatively integrate rapidly growing alternative delivery system components of the product line into carefully selected locations.

As alternatives to the acute care setting are identified, a variety of opportunities are available to the hospital. In some cases, the facility may decide to initiate an alternate delivery site as a hospital sponsored project or as a joint venture with the medical staff. In highly competitive markets or in situations where the hospital does not wish to participate in a delivery alternative, the medical staff may identify a new "place."

The ramifications of hospital-sponsored, physician-sponsored or joint venture projects obviously must be considered seriously during the market planning process. Without their involvement in product line market planning, physicians who have traditionally been coproviders may become competitors to preserve their own financial interest. In many cases, hospitals may find that a joint venture on a delivery alternative may result in a low financial return at the new delivery site but preserve the high profit margin on inpatient care by preventing the alienation of actively admitting physicians. Hospitals that have built trust relationships between administration and the medical staff through the active involvement of physicians in product line market planning will be much more successful in structuring joint venture agreements that preserve a center of excellence's profit margin than will facilities which have viewed all physicians as adversaries.

Financing decisions can be market driven or driven by the hospital's finance department. Using either method, the hospital must first determine its own costs for delivering services within the product line. Market driven pricing then uses a comparison of competitors' pricing structures as the foundation for your pricing strategy. If your own costs for providing a service are lower than your competitor's prices, you may be successful in negotiating a lower contract rate with an HMO or PPO. In some cases it may even be advantageous to enter the market as the "low price alternative." Your research can help determine price sensitivity or whether a low or premium price strategy would be a good position to adopt with your selected target audiences. Without knowledge of the specific costs of delivering services within the product line, it is difficult to achieve the marketing purpose.

Finance department pricing strategies rely solely on the hospital's cost of delivering a service to determine what pricing structure should be used.

Obviously, finance department input into any pricing strategy is important. Sometimes the facility will identify market driven pricing and finance department-driven pricing and find the two vary greatly. If the finance department's recommendations are lower than what the market place will bear, this is an opportunity to increase the profit margin for the particular product line, or enter the market as the low cost provider. However, if the finance projections are much higher than what your research determines the market will bear, a rethinking of the initial marketing mission of the product line may be necessary.

The last step in creating the marketing mix is developing promotional strategies. Again, referring to the positioning strategies developed for each target audience, specific promotional strategies should be developed for individual external and internal target audiences. Successfully designed research will assist in identifying promotional vehicles which will most successfully reach each target audience. Then you will know if a particular product, program or service is physician driven or consumer driven. It is not at all cost effective to try to "sell" a product line which is physician driven through advertising aimed at the consuming public.

Research in some markets shows that obstetrical services are particularly sensitive to product attributes which are promoted directly to the consuming public. However, in other markets consumers say their hospital choice for obstetrics is driven by their prior selection of a health plan and a physician who participates in their plan. Research can help determine what type of market you are in.

The acute phases of heart and cancer care are obviously physician driven. However, educational, rehabilitation and support phases are much more sensitive to direction by the consuming public. Research still shows that cancer and heart patients and their family members rely heavily on physician recommendations to access all components of the health care continuum.

Just as this is not a book on research, the goal of this book is not to provide a primer or advanced text on promotional strategies, including public relations and advertising. However, some key points alluded to previously bear repeating:

- Promotional strategies and promotional vehicles should be identified for each internal and external target audience. The brochure which works well in informing the physician's office staff about a new service cannot take the place of a newspaper ad or television spot directed at the consumer public. The same promotional materials probably cannot be used for physicians on your staff already admitting to the product line and referring physicians who are unfamiliar with your services. Although targeted promotional activities may result in a wider range of promotional vehicles, they will zero in on each market segment and will certainly be more effective than a single generic piece.

- The impact of public relations and paid advertising on internal audiences should not be overlooked. Even if it is determined that the consumer for a specific product line is the physician and not a member of the public, the hospital may want to create image advertising or public relations strategies that focus on the particular product line. This is a route to consider particularly if competitive hospitals and alternative delivery systems are publicly promoting a specific program or service. However, if media public relations and advertising is being done with the medical staff and employees as the target audience, make sure that you are achieving your objectives with these audiences. This can be done by featuring employees and physicians in the promotional pieces, previewing advertising for physicians and employees and prominently posting ads on internal bulletin boards.

- Targeted promotional programs are not necessarily "cheap." By working with your marketing mix and determining which target audiences will have the greatest impact on your product line, you can determine what promotional strategies will be most cost effective and what strategies should be used to meet other internal and external objectives. Again, it is important to identify who are your competitors for various promotional vehicles. If television advertising is the selected medium, realize that your ad is competing for attention with the multimillion dollar budgets of Pepsi, Coke and E.F. Hutton. If physician promotion is the route you want to take think for a moment about all of the printed materials your physicians receive every day. Maybe money can be more wisely spent by investing in a physician liaison who personally visits the doctor's office and talks to the physician and his/her office staff than in "another brochure."

O = OBJECTIVES

You've established a purpose, completed your research and set the marketing mix. This next step will determine whether the marketing plan sits on a shelf to gather dust or is implemented.

Before completing the marketing plan, translate the marketing mix into action oriented measurable objec-

LĬTH·Ō

The Forefront of Quality Medical Care

We're proud to announce the introduction of Extracorporeal Shock-Wave Lithotripsy as a new feature of our kidney stone treatment program at CAMC's High Tech Center. Now you have the opportunity to participate in this state-of-the-art procedure.

As you know, lithotripsy is a revolutionary new technology which breaks up kidney stones non-invasively. The process is less painful, entails fewer side effects, and recuperation is quicker than with conventional surgery. It's even less expensive than surgery. This is truly the wave of the future in the treatment of kidney stones.

The theory behind lithotripsy is simple: shock waves shatter and eventually disintegrate kidney stones into sand-like particles that are washed out in the urine.

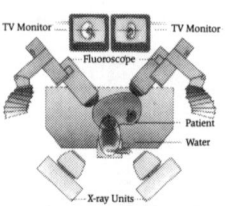

The first step in the procedure is to pinpoint the location of the stone inside the body. Using the TV monitors, the shock waves are centered on the stone with fluoroscopy and treatment can begin.

The lithotripter is synchronized with the patient's heartbeat by electrocardiogram. The machine is activated to fire on every R wave if the heart rate is less than 120 beats per minute. If the heart rate is above 120, the machine fires on alternate R waves. This synchronization avoids interference with the heart's conduction system.

The stone is examined by fluoroscopy throughout the procedure. When necessary, the patient can be repositioned for maximum effect. The whole process is supervised by the physician who controls all of the firing sequences with a switch. Usually, the entire process takes about an hour.

Benefits to Kidney Stone Sufferers

As you know, medical research has shown that the southern region of the United States has a higher rate of kidney stone disease than other parts of the country. In fact, our part of the country has been named "The Stone Belt" by researchers.

Lithotripsy has been endorsed by the FDA and the majority of the urological community.

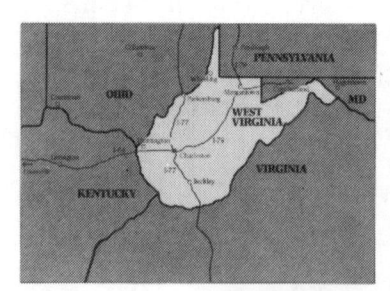

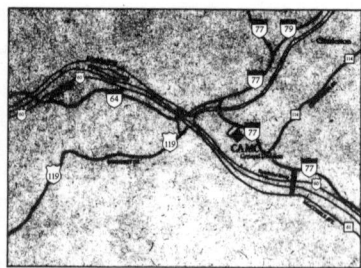

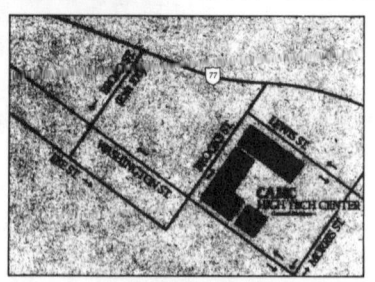

CAMC
Charleston Area Medical Center
1-800-654-0159

We Care For West Virginia

L·I·T·H·O·TRĬP·SY

according to the U.S. Department of Health and Human Services, 90% of all kidney stone cases can be successfully treated with this new method.

Clearly, lithotripsy is on the cutting edge in kidney stone treatment—but there's no actual cutting involved. This is the primary benefit offered by this new process. As a result, patients experience less pain and fewer post-operative risks.

Further, lithotripsy is less expensive than conventional surgery. Since the time needed for recuperation following lithotripsy is only two or three days (as you know, the average stay for surgery is ten days), the patient saves time and money on the hospital stay. Overall, lithotripsy costs less than surgery.

All the same, certain precautions must be observed in designating patients for lithotripsy. Patients are not recommended for lithotripsy if their weight exceeds 300 pounds or if their height is less than 4 feet or more than 6 feet, 6 inches. There are additional risks if the kidney with the stone has little or no function or if there is an uncontrolled urinary infection. Often, cardiac problems disallow lithotripsy therapy as will any significant obstruction distal to the stone.

Looking to the Future at CAMC

Placement of a lithotripter at CAMC's new High Tech Center at the Medical Center's downtown General Division represents CAMC's continuing commitment to remain at the forefront of quality medical care. CAMC physicians, nurses and technicians are dedicated to providing state-of-the-art care to those in our region who need it.

How You Can Participate in a New Era

We invite you to visit CAMC and see the lithotripter in action. Learn about this revolutionary therapy which is changing the face of kidney stone treatment. We will be happy to send you brochures on lithotripsy for use by your patients as well.

We're encouraging all area urologists to apply for privileges in Extracorporeal Shock-Wave Lithotripsy. We've recently amended our bylaws to accommodate interested urologists as members of the medical staff in lithotripsy and the management of lithotripsy patients. Call CAMC for more information about the criteria for certification in lithotripsy.

At CAMC, "We Care For West Virginia" is more than just a phrase. It's a commitment.

For more information about lithotripsy and our kidney stone treatment program, call CAMC at 1-800-654-0159.

CAMC
Charleston Area Medical Center
1-800-654-0159
We Care For West Virginia

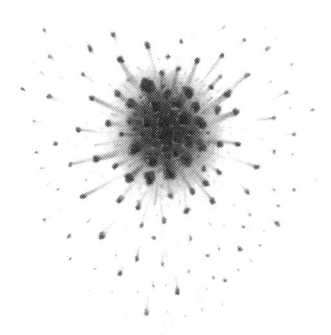

Pulverizing Renal Calculi.

The cutting edge in non-invasive treatment.

This brochure was developed to make CAMC physicians and physicians throughout CAMC's referral territory aware of the new lithotripsy capabilities. Medical Journal ads complemented the brochure. Provided courtesy of McDonald Davis and Associates, a Milwaukee-based firm specializing in healthcare marketing communications, research, promotion and planning.

tives—just as you have done with management by objectives (MBO) for years. Write action oriented "to do" statements, assign the responsibility for implementing the objective to someone on your staff and develop an implementation time frame.

Physicians who have been involved in the market-based planning phases of your project should also be involved in this objective setting step. It is important to involve department heads and employees at this phase to determine what internal road blocks may exist to implementing specific marketing objectives.

For example, if your research shows consumers are interested in a variety of obstetrical anesthesia options and your medical staff is supportive of 24 hour in-house anesthesia, do not promote this service until you have successfully recruited anesthesiologists or nurse anesthetists to staff it. In some locations, you may find that the recruitment of a new clinical specialist may take many weeks or months. It is always best to build in enough time to ensure that new procedures are working smoothly before they are promoted. Remember, "You only get one chance to make a first impression." It seems hard to believe, but it is a standard of communications theory that one dissatisfied customer will lead to 200 people knowing about the bad experience within 24 hours while someone who is pleased with a product or service is likely to let as few as seven people know.

Some of your objectives may require regulatory approvals, capital financing or special fund raising efforts. Once marketing plans are initially developed, their updates should be done to coincide with your hospital's regular budgeting process so financing of product line marketing objectives is considered along with other operational issues of the hospital.

The need for regulatory approvals or capital financing does not mean that marketing activity remains at a standstill while approvals or financing are sought. The time lag provides an excellent opportunity to expand the physician, employee and patient data base, to integrate additional physicians into the product line marketing process, and to build trust between administration and the medical staff as physicians see that their involvement really does make a difference.

e = EVALUATION

Yes 'e' is a small letter. This is a special reminder to the marketing task force that although PRIMOe is not typically spelled with an 'e', that evaluating the success of market plan implementation is vital to the entire process.

Evaluation mechanisms should be in place before the marketing plan is finally implemented to ensure data needed to measure success or failure is being collected and will be meaningful.

If patient satisfaction levels have been measured as part of the initial research, periodic resurveying of discharged patients will tell you if guest relations objectives are being met. Continuous monitoring of secondary data regarding physician activity and patient origin studies will tell you how successful your objectives have been in reaching specific members of your medical staff and how successful your referral area promotional efforts are.

Every ad, every publication, every educational class and every new piece of equipment should be evaluated to determine if the objectives for printing the publication or buying the piece of equipment are being met.

Evaluation mechanisms do not have to be expensive, but they must be consistently used if the success of a marketing plan is to be measured over time.

Just as you have involved physicians throughout the

market planning process, it is important that they are involved in this evaluation step. Continually solicit their input using one-on-one interviews, physician focus groups or multidisciplinary focus groups; track their admitting activity, and, on a less formal basis, ask them how things are going. This will add to your credibility and positively reinforce their participation in the product line marketing process.

SOME QUESTIONS AND ANSWERS

How can I involve my physician competitors in the product line marketing process?

Physicians can be categorized as coproviders, patient brokers and competitors. Coproviders include the traditional hospital based physicians like anesthesiologists, radiologists and pathologists as well as newer subspecialists such as perinatologists, neonatologists and subspecialty cancer surgeons who rely heavily on the hospital for their own success. Patient brokers make up the bulk of a medical staff and include those physicians with privileges at competitive hospitals who make admitting decisions based on their patients' needs. Competitors include ophthalmologists with their own surgery suites and lasers in their offices, surgeons with their own free standing surgery centers, as well as radiologists with CT scanners and MRI capability in their offices and cardiologists considering the development of free-standing cath labs, etc. Obviously, you do not want competitors involved in strategic market planning discussions. Physicians participating in the strategy stages of market planning should be coproviders and the most loyal patient brokers. However, there is no reason why competitors and all patient brokers cannot participate in the research process.

How can I avoid problems and build trust among the medical staff through product line market planning?

Perhaps the key to trust building is feedback and honesty. If you involve the physicians in the research process you need to be prepared to listen to what they have to say and respond to their suggestions and concerns. That does not mean that all their suggestions must be implemented, but you need to be prepared to tell them why certain suggestions were not used. The research process itself builds expectations among the medical staff that you will listen and will provide feedback.

Will product line marketing even matter once everyone is covered by capitation or other forms of contracting?

The premise that not all institutions can be all things to all people suggests that capitation and other forms of contracting, whether by service, admission, day, diagnostic group, or some other unit, will vary in scope, complexity, cost, and price. As long as contracting remains pluralistic and negotiable, marketing will be essential for its success. Marketing a particular product line recognizes the organization's strengths and weaknesses to respond to a contracting niche or to create a contracting niche based on how it focuses its resources and expertise. Even total, or "pure" capitation would produce layers of subcontracting in order to complete the service scope—and the effectiveness of the subcontracting would be reflective of the market position of the hospital.

How can I evaluate the effectiveness of my product line marketing effort?

The two key ways are physician attitudes and financial performance. They are directly related.

The success of product line marketing can be evaluated by tracking physician referrals, physician utilization and physician satisfaction. You can repeat the research process, look at admitting statistics, and formally or informally ask your physicians how they think things are going.

You also can evaluate the return on investment of your marketing efforts. Have community promotional activities resulted in greater participation in educational screening and prevention activities? Have information and physician referral services resulted in increased referrals to your physicians? And, is there increased awareness of your center of excellence? Has targeting of your physician and community promotion led to a more favorable payor mix? All of these questions lead to a need for a discussion of cost accounting and its impact on product lines. The bottom line of the effectiveness of product line marketing is the achievement of the financial objectives in the form of the operating margin of the product line. The operating margin of the hospital is generated by the established accounting system, and the operating margin of the product line needs to be based on the cost accounting detail comprising the product line. As discussed earlier, the product lines are dynamic and many times overlap, which creates cost accounting inconsistencies and allocation ambiguity. However, without good cost accounting data by product line, true operating margin tracking cannot occur. The solution is an automated cost accounting model by department, whereby each department manager learns to "cost up" each service component comprising his contribution to the product line. It means that each department manager needs to know the incremental, direct cost of each service, as well as the "fully loaded" and economic cost of each service. The product line manager, in turn, rolls up each department manager's portion of costs which make up that product line. With this information, tailored product lines can be established with a basis to set and achieve product line operating margin performance objectives.

Trust Building

Involving physicians in the product line market planning process can pay dividends far beyond the formalization of marketing plans. It can set the stage for a whole new environment in which the hospital and the medical staff work together to accomplish mutually beneficial goals. These benefits are a logical extension of the models which have been discussed in preceding chapters and the examples of how physicians can be involved in the development of product line marketing plans for a variety of clinical services. However, the importance of this trust building role for physician involvement in product line marketing planning requires emphasis and the development of specific examples.

Formal Settings

Physician involvement in the planning process is a prime way to get "buy in" from the doctors. If they're involved in the planning process they are more likely to be supportive of the plan's implementation. For example:

- Physicians are involved in the development of an OB marketing plan. Research with consumers and the medical staff indicates the hospital has a good reputation but doctors are not desirous of increasing their OB patient loads. This points directly to the need for physician recruitment in this area. Doctors who are involved in the planning process are much more likely not only to be supportive of this recruitment effort but also help sell it to others on the medical staff. Perhaps they will even be directly involved in adding new physicians to their practices or identifying doctors interested in moving to your community or your hospital.

- Physicians are active participants on a cardiac product line marketing task force. Secondary research indicates the need for expansion of the hospital's cardiac catheterization facilities to meet increasing local demands as well as to support a new regionalization approach. The hospital's present physical facility cannot support this expansion. Following presentation on the feasibility and examples of free standing cath labs the physicians on the marketing task force recommend the establishment of a free standing facility and suggest it be developed as a joint venture between interested cardiologists and the hospital.

- Research with past geriatric patients indicates the need for guest relations training and transportation to and from physician's office appointments. In working with physicians involved in a geriatric marketing task force the suggestion is made that physicians can attract additional geriatric patients to their practices if they are viewed as being responsive to consumers' needs. The task force asks the hospital's marketing department to prepare a program for physician practice enhancement which can be offered to all primary care physicians on the medical staff. The physicians on the task force even offer to test the system in their own offices to aid the practice enhancement efforts.

Research which forms the foundation of a product line marketing plan can facilitate the trust building process. The administrative staff which is not afraid to ask for physician opinions and then provide feedback is definitely seen as more responsive than an administrative staff which acts unilaterally.

There are several ways in which the presentation of research findings can be used as a trust building tool with the medical staff:

- Once research is completed, the consultant who has conducted the research can present medical findings to medical staff groups in a confidential manner with no administrative representatives present.
- A better alternative is for the consultant to present research findings and then have administrative representatives lead a discussion of the implications of the research with medical staff members present.
- The trust building implications can be expanded to the Board if the presentation of research find-

ings is done preliminary to a less structured social interchange with administrators, Board members and key physicians with their spouses present. Carefully selecting the appropriate couples who should sit together at small tables of eight or ten is key to the success of this type of feedback and trust building opportunity. In this less formal setting, it is possible to discuss the philosophy and implications of the research without delving so deeply into the implementation implications. This type of trust building session, however, is dependent upon all players understanding their appropriate role. The Board members must remember that their role is *not* to make operational decisions. They should be prepared to solicit input in this informal social setting and have a planned means of communicating this to the administrative staff. This type of session can be instrumental in breaking down barriers between "us" and "them."

An informal approach

Trust building, of course, is an ongoing process and an important objective of every administrator when dealing with the medical staff. It is worth noting, therefore, that a setting which is the direct opposite of formalized task force meetings or even structured social occasions is available to every administrator: the doctors' lounge in the hospital.

The administrator who makes a commitment to visiting the physicians' lounge every day has an opportunity to interact with doctors when both they and the administrator are in a variety of moods. That can help build personal as well as professional relationships. Successfully "managing in the physicians' lounge" requires flexibility, since there will be no agenda for the interactions. Marketing can become the subject of discussion as naturally as anything else.

A busy administrator may question the priority of spending time in the physicians' lounge. Doctors, however, never seem to ask why an administrator would want to get to know the medical staff. And it rarely occurs to a physician that the administrator could be doing anything better than establishing communications channels and building trust with the medical staff. They could be right.

Patient Research

What's ahead for the hospital which has fully integrated physicians into the product line market planning process? How can you hope to continue to be on the cutting edge? What can you do differently as your competitors get on the bandwagon and begin involving physicians in the product line marketing process?

To date, the research which forms the foundation for the product line marketing process has been heavily weighted towards the physician. After all, it is the doctor who admits patients to the hospital. The next generation of responsiveness, however, is with the consumer. This is not to say that the hospital's clinical product lines will become ones in which the consumer admits himself for open heart surgery or herself to have a baby. Rather, both physicians and hospitals are becoming more conscious of consumer choice as competition heats up. With a growing pool of available physicians, consumers are realizing they do have choices even in many small communities. Therefore, the doctors become concerned about their own responsiveness to patient needs and demands. The patient research base can be another trust building joint venture opportunity for the hospital and the medical staff.

Objectives

There are essentially two objectives of patient research: public relations and management decision making. The public relations benefit of patient research is obtained when every patient receives some type of satisfaction assessment. Typically, however, unless distribution and return is carefully controlled, the hospital does not obtain a sample of sufficient size to quantify the results and hold department managers accountable for actions. Enter the mailed survey with a sufficient response, the telephone survey and focus groups.

Public relations is, obviously, a major objective of patient satisfaction research. Perhaps the hospital does want to distribute a very brief "post card" survey to everyone who is discharged. Ideally, this is mailed to the patient, but if the cost of that is prohibitive based on the large number of discharges or the small size of the public relations budget, the "post card survey" could be distributed by the business office at discharge or in the room by housekeeping or by a volunteer discharge escort. The public relations survey would perhaps ask five key questions:

- What was your overall impression of the nursing care you received?

- What was your overall impression of the food you were served?
- What was your overall impression of the cleanliness of your room and other areas of the hospital you visited?
- What was your overall impression of your hospital stay?
- If you need to be hospitalized again, would you return to this same hospital and recommend it to others?

The quantitative survey which produces a random and large enough sample to make it meaningful for management purposes is considerably different. First of all, it is probably much longer. Patients seem to be willing to respond to questionnaires of 30 to 35 carefully written, multiple choice questions. They usually will also write in comments to one or two open ended questions. Past obstetrical patients are willing to respond to a greater number of questions, perhaps as many as 50. Questions need to be carefully worded and based on key management measures of quality, i.e., When you pressed your nurse call button, did someone respond right away? Did personnel caring for you introduce themselves? *Were procedures explained in terms you could understand?*, and so on. Obviously, it is important to involve managers in the design of the questions if it is expected they will be responsive to the results. Similarly, if the questionnaire is to contain questions about the patient's interactions with his or her physician while in the hospital, the medical staff needs to be involved in questionnaire design, too. The hospital's quality assurance committee is, typically, an appropriate group to recruit for this purpose.

The best responses to patient questionnaires of this type are seen when the questionnaire is mailed to the patient following discharge. This is the easiest way to control distribution and ensure questionnaires are sent to every patient during a particular month or quarter or to randomly selected patients during this time period. Response rates of 20 to 60% can be obtained easily if the questionnaires are mailed to the patients within a week or so following discharge. The more rapidly the questionnaires are mailed, the better the response rates will be. Hospitals that depend on the business, admitting, volunteer or housekeeping departments or any other internal staff members to "remember" to give each patient a questionnaire, find their response rates are considerably lower.

Obviously, the questionnaire is mailed with a cover letter explaining the purpose of the survey and a wish from the hospital that the patient is on the road to recovery. The letter can be signed by an administrator, vice president of marketing, or perhaps even a physician. The title of the signator should be meaningful to the patient. The director of quality control may be an important person in your hospital's heirarchy, but what does quality control mean to the patient—they *expect* quality.

USING THE DATA

The key to successfully using quantitative patient satisfaction data for management decision making purposes is to keep it timely. Questionnaires must be received from a sufficient sample of patients in a month or quarter to warrant tabulation and analysis of results. Ideally, a sample size of at least 200 questionnaires are returned before this analysis occurs. A detailed report should then be written and distributed to administrative staff, department heads and medical staff. The hospital which conducts quantifiable patient satisfaction research on an ongoing basis is in a position to have administrative staff work with department heads in developing performance standards for which the manager is held accountable. For example, if, after baseline research is conducted, the administrative staff and department heads agree that all departments will achieve a 90% to 95% satisfaction rating in future surveys, department heads have a standard to work for. If the department head consistently falls below this standard, corrective action should occur.

Quantitative patient satisfaction surveys, obviously, are needed to develop management decision making tools, but multiple choice questions, percentages and statistics do not really provide a flavor for the patient's true feelings about the hospital. This can only be done through qualitative research. Focus groups conducted with past patients can provide valuable information about the care they received, their attitudes about this care and what they are telling others.

The focus group facilitator should be prepared with a list of questions that will elicit responses regarding all aspects of the patient's care, from admitting to nursing services, from ancillary support to discharge and billing. Specific questions should be asked about the food, the cleanliness of the hospital, parking accommodations for visitors and experiences in surgery. Involving the physicians in the qualitative research process, questions can also include issues such as satisfaction with their doctor's presence during their hospitalization, the presurgical information they received, the role of the assisting surgeon and satisfaction with anesthesia.

Because focus group comments are recorded verbatim, the report which is developed during a series of these qualitative sessions provides a much more definitive flavor of the patient's actual satisfaction or lack of satisfaction with the hospital experience.

Technology makes it possible to carry this process

one step further. Some hospitals may choose to hold patient satisfaction focus groups in a facility designed for this purpose. A one-way mirror provides an opportunity for hospital representatives to actually observe the focus groups. When this is not possible or when most administrators and department heads are unwilling to sit through many hours of sessions with past patients, these focus groups can be recorded on videotape. It is easy to produce a tape when using a focus group facility because the participants can not see the camera. However, even if past patient focus groups are held in the hospital or in another community location, videotaping can be done. Most people are so used to seeing video cameras, they are not overly intimidated by this process. A good facilitator will have them speaking and not worrying about the video camera within a few minutes.

The greatest benefit from videotaping qualitative focus groups is seen when the videotapes are edited to support the conclusions drawn by the facilitator's report. For example, if following a series of six or ten past patient focus groups, the facilitator identified eight or ten key summarizing points, actual patient comments which have been recorded on videotape can be edited to support these findings. The resulting videotapes should not be longer than 20 or 30 minutes. This provides a powerful communications tool when the facilitator or marketing director is presenting the focus group findings to the hospital's executive staff, physicians or department heads. It is hard for a physician to argue the fact that patients are resentful of bills from assistant surgeons they never meet or anesthesiologists who never introduce themselves when you have comments from 10 to 12 patients on videotape.

Similarly, the nursing director will find it hard to argue that he or she has a problem with IV therapy when the actual comments from patients in every focus group have been edited to tell in their personal words the difficulties nurses had starting IVs.

The hospital with the best opportunities to develop a consumer-driven set of patient satisfaction standards for both the hospital and the physician's practice is, obviously, the facility which combines quantitative and qualitative methodologies to develop an integrated patient satisfaction data base. Qualitative research can be used to probe in depth about trends which are seen in the quantitative surveys and can be used to establish specific standards for evaluating employee and department head performance.

Extending the research base

The most dramatic extension of this research base, however, is seen when the focus group sessions are used to identify a series of patient satisfaction standards in the doctors' office practices and for the hospital. These standards are then adhered to. They become the basis for physician referral services and consumer advertising. This is where the patient satisfaction process becomes integrated with the product line marketing process.

For example, the hospital is developing a product line marketing plan for its OB Department or women's center. The initial feeling may be that the women's center needs to be a primary care clinic staffed by female practitioners or that the hospital's recruiting needs to focus solely on female obstetricians. Although this may be ideal, in most communities, it would have a negative impact on existing relationships with the hospital's predominantly male OB/Gyn medical staff members.

Qualitative and quantitative research indicates that although many women enjoy seeing female practitioners, the sex of their doctor is not nearly as important to them as the doctor's communications skills and office procedures. Therefore, using focus group research, specific *consumer driven patient satisfaction* standards are identified for a doctor's office practice and the hospital.

A series of 10 or 15 standards is identified as important in an office practice based on input from consumers participating in six focus groups of women planning to have children in the next two years. These standards are then discussed with the medical staff to determine if there is anything medically or legally inconsistent with their adoption. If not, they become the standards for physicians who want to be part of an OB/Gyn physician referral service. The doctor must sign off that he or she agrees to abide by these consumer driven patient satisfaction standards. These might be standards such as not keeping the woman waiting more than 15 minutes for an appointment, discussing anesthesia options with her, allowing her husband to be present for delivery, even if she has a C-section, etc. The hospital then can promote or advertise that physicians participating in its physician referral service have agreed to abide by these consumer driven patient satisfaction standards. Ongoing monitoring of compliance with these standards can be done through repeated focus groups and patient satisfaction surveys conducted by the doctor's office using survey instruments that identify these specific standards.

The same principles can apply to consumer driven patient satisfaction standards for the hospital's OB unit. Focus groups again can be used to identify 10 or 15 key determinants of patient satisfaction or quality of care. The hospital then ensures these standards. For example: Providing a bonding time for mother, father and baby, unless medically contraindicated; providing optional rooming-in arrangements, and not allowing smoking in any patient rooms, but identifying a smoking lounge on the OB floor. It is, again, easy to see that these standards can be used in marketing communications materials designed to promote the unit.

Even in obstetrics, in which many patients say they do select their hospital before picking a physician who will deliver their baby, the development and implementation of consumer driven patient satisfaction standards cannot be achieved successfully unless both the hospital and the doctor participate in the process. Many key points of satisfaction with the delivery process involve the physician's role in the hospital and cannot be implemented unilaterally by the facility, e.g., fathers in delivery rooms for C-sections, use of alternative birth center or LDR (labor/delivery/recovery) rooms, etc. The ongoing evaluation of hospital based consumer driven patient satisfaction standards is, obviously, done through the research process discussed earlier.

In a more tertiary and clinically oriented product line, the "consumers" for a particular product line may not be the general public and patients, but rather, referring physicians. A tertiary heart center is perhaps a good example of this. Patients, obviously, do not admit themselves for cardiac catheterization or open heart surgery, but typically, they do not seek out a cardiologist or cardiovascular surgeon themselves either. They are referred to this person by their primary care physician or another specialist who determines they have or might have a heart problem. The same type of research described for the general consumer and past patient then is done with referring physicians from the hospital's own medical staff and in a regional referral area. Again, the research is done to identify and assess quality standards which primary physicians feel must be adhered to if they are going to continue to refer patients to your hospital's cardiologists and cardiovascular surgeons.

Primary care physicians on your own hospital's medical staff can be surveyed through focus groups and individual interviews in their offices. If referring physicians are from a large geographic area, it may not be feasible to conduct in-person research. It may be necessary to conduct research on the telephone or by mail. However, if your facility does receive a large number of referrals from a specific community outside of your primary service area, it may be worthwhile to schedule one or two focus groups with physicians in that area to obtain their actual comments. There is nothing like the personal touch!

It is not usually recommended that physician research sessions be audio or videotape recorded. However, if the sole purpose of physician research is to establish quality standards, the doctors may, indeed, be candid even while taping. If you suspect the physicians—particularly those on your own staff—will not be completely candid if recording devices are used, it would be better to eliminate this step. You can rely on a facilitator who uses another method of recording, but still is able to capture specific comments which can be incorporated in a report.

Standards which might be developed using this process would include feedback from the tertiary specialists, return of the patient to the primary care physician's control, continuing education opportunities and family education, etc. Compliance with these standards, obviously, is measured through repeat research with the referring physicians and patient satisfaction research with the people they have referred.

Again, the development and implementation of these standards can be used in marketing communications vehicles for a physician-driven service such as a heart center. However, these marketing communications vehicles are probably more likely to be newsletters, continuing education sessions and speaker's bureau presentations rather than advertisements in the local or regional media.

Summary

Consumer driven patient satisfaction standards like those described for OB can be used in the development of a product line in which the general public has a major decision making role. These would include OB, urgent care centers, emergency departments, sports medicine and some rehab programs. When the physician is the primary decision maker, a process similar to that described for the heart center should be used. Developing standards for programs like heart, cancer, neurosciences and orthopedics would be examples of this format.

This is a new concept and, perhaps, will be viewed as revolutionary by administrators, department heads and surely, physicians. However, it is consistent with calls by all of these groups, employers and the Joint Commission on Accreditation of Hospitals for ways to define quality in the eyes of the hospital's target audiences. The doctor or administrator must be concerned with the development of patient care plans and procedures in the operating room which ensure that all instruments are accounted for. When patient research shows clearly that cleanliness and good food are important to the patient, even doctors and administrators must be concerned with the quality of these services, too. Quality, just like any marketing position statement, is seen through the eyes of the target audience. The administrator, the doctor, the patient and the family member all have different standards of quality. Qualitative and quantitative research can help identify these standards and enable the hospital to maintain a competitive edge.

More Questions and More Answers

The questions and answers at the end of chapters 1 and 2 refer specifically to material in those chapters. The questions originally were posed by a panel of administrators, marketing directors and physicians who have reviewed this book. Their names appear in chapter 1, and the authors express their gratitude for the reviewers' time and concern.

Those aren't, however, the only questions we've been asked about physician involvement in product line marketing. Another source of questions has been the audiences for the presentations we have made around the country. The balance of this chapter consists of additional queries about the subject and our answers.

QUESTIONS AND ANSWERS

If you have an open medical staff, how do you create economic ties with your physicians?

The process of governing the medical staff should be separate from any business relationships the hospital has with its physicians. If the medical staff is an open one, it is vital that the hospital pick and choose its business partners carefully.

If you have categorized your physicians as coproviders, competitors and patient brokers you may be concerned about suggesting joint business ventures with physicians who are competitors. Perhaps, however, the nature of the physician's competition with the hospital is different than the nature of the proposed business venture. If this is the case, it may be possible for physicians who are competitors on one hand to be business partners on another. This can help build financial ties between the hospital and its medical staff members. Obviously, if the hospital is to enter into a business deal with a physician competitor, or potential competitor, everyone must be very clear on the specific nature of the business dealings.

Sometimes it is also advantageous to involve a variety of physicians in a business deal or joint venture. For example, if the hospital is proposing a joint venture opportunity to develop a free standing cath lab, the offering should not be made solely to physicians connected with the hospital's heart program. The facility may find that some internal medicine specialists are also interested in the project as a business venture. Sometimes having physicians from more than one specialty can pro vide a sense of balance to the joint venture. For that reason the development of a business opportunity to build and operate a surgery center might be offered to anesthesiologists and surgeons instead of just one group or the other.

How do you create fiduciary relationships with your medical staff?

Although that perhaps could be the topic of an entire new book, some key caveats may be helpful to the hospital embarking upon product line marketing.

Perhaps the most important step to take in establishing fiduciary relationships with your medical staff is for both parties to have a clear understanding of what each wants to achieve. What are the hospital's goals? Are you trying to capture market share, provide a balance for contracting, or is bottom line financial return your primary objective? Similarly, what are the physicians' goals? Are they looking for a return on investments, tax write off, professional gratification, or even the belief that the joint venture can produce a "better" product?

Who should chair the product line marketing task force?

The scenario discussed in the book suggests that an administrative representative with responsibility for the product line area is an appropriate task force chair. Support for the task force is provided by administration, marketing and the clinical coordinator or administrative director of the specific product line. An alternative scenario is suggested by Bill Murray at St. Vincent's Hospital in Billings, Montana, a member of the book's review panel. St. Vincent's has been very successful in appointing physician chairs of product line marketing committees or task forces. Although the administrator still drives the process and coordinates all staff work, having a physician chair adds credibility to the process and results in greater ownership of the resulting marketing plan by members of the medical staff.

What is the ideal size for a focus group?

Customarily focus groups are made up of 10 to 12 participants. This is an ideal number for employee, consumer or past patient focus groups but may be too high for physician sessions. Six to eight physicians actively participating in a qualitative research forum mean the focus group facilitator is *very busy.*

Normally, focus groups with grass roots employees last 60 to 90 minutes. Focus groups with supervisors and administrative coordinators can last 90 minutes to 2 hours. Consumer and past patient focus groups normally will last almost two hours. However, senior citizens respond better if the groups are limited to 90 minutes. Physician focus groups, on the other hand, are normally scheduled for 90 minutes but the facilitator is lucky if most of the physician participants are in attendance at least 60 minutes. This is another reason a smaller number of participants is adequate for this audience.

How has the new competitive market place changed pricing strategies?

In the past there was a feeling that the low price strategy was probably one which hospitals *did not* want to adopt. There was a feeling that in the mind of many consumers, low price and low quality were synonymous and no one wanted to be positioned as the low quality health care provider. However, as contracting negotiations with HMO's, PPO's and insurance companies expand, the low price strategy may be the only successful strategy for a health care facility to adopt. This is particularly true if you are negotiating with a health plan or a government agency which sincerely believes that quality is comparable among all local providers.

Hospitals today are finding they must have more than one price differentiation strategy from their competitors. They, perhaps, need a different price differentiation for *each* potential contractor. The strategy is based on the contractor's knowledge of the health care market place and willingness to pay a price differential for services which are qualitatively different.

With the defending of health system agencies and many statewide offices of health planning, secondary research data is becoming less and less available. How can the hospital cope?

Not only are many agencies being defunded, but some are losing their authority to collect data and share this information with facilities that have become dependent on competitive market place statistics. Obviously, hospitals can still rely on primary research data available through quantitative or qualitative research methodologies. Physicians who are patient brokers can sometimes provide a wealth of information about pricing strategies and comparisons with your competitors. Although consumer research may not provide completely accurate pricing comparisons among competitors, the perceptions offered by consumers and past patients can be very valuable. For example, if it is the perception of general consumers and past patients that you are the high priced provider and this is driving business to your competitor, a more in-depth analysis may be needed.

As hospitals throughout the country are seeking to be more consumer responsive, price shopping by telephone can also provide valuable information. Simply call a competitor's business office and ask how much it would cost to have a baby at the facility. It is also a good idea to do this same anonymous shopping with your own business office to see how accurate the information is which you are providing.

In some areas, the state hospital association or regional hospital council continues to collect and publish comparative utilization data. More sophisticated computer systems are making this data available more readily and more rapidly.

The physicians' marketing task force described in the book can easily be adapted to a subspecialty product line like a heart center. Are there any general guidelines on how to select doctors for the physician marketing task force model?

There are two basic rules for the successful establishment of any physician marketing task force: Don't overlook the role of the primary care physician and have a clear understanding of the various levels of physician referral before selecting task force participants.

Even if the marketing task force is being formed to guide the development of a marketing plan for a tertiary product line like a heart center or a cancer center, do not limit the physician task force participants to subspecialists. These physicians receive their patients through referral by primary care physicians and the input of generalists will be vital to the success of the marketing plan. In looking at the various levels of physician referral, typically primary care physicians refer to diagnostic specialists and they in turn refer to therapeutic members of the medical staff. Each of these referring groups should be represented on the task force.

Perhaps another example would be helpful. If you are developing a market plan for an obstetrical or perinatal center, be sure to include family practice physicians who refer to obstetricians, family practice physicians who do some obstetrics themselves, and obstetricians on your staff as well as perinatologists and neonatologists who are coproviders. If you are establishing a physician marketing task force to assist in the development of a marketing plan for a diabetes center, be sure to include endocrinologists and primary care physicians who see many of your diabetic patients, but also look to other specialists who see patients with complications of diabetes, for example, ophthalmologists.

Marketing is in vogue in today's hospital. Yet many members of the medical staff still assume marketing and advertising are synonymous. Is there an easy way to describe marketing to the medical staff?

Marketing, and particularly product line marketing, is nothing more than the application of sound business fundamentals in the health care arena. Since many members of the medical staff do not have business backgrounds, perhaps it would be appropriate to liken the marketing process to the scientific method, which was the foundation of their clinical training. In the marketing process, we identify a purpose or goal, proceed with research, formalize the structure of a marketing mix including product and pricing decisions, use marketing communications to tell our customers about the product we have available, and then evaluate our marketing program to determine how well we have responded to the needs of our target audiences. That essentially is what the scientific method is all about, too. The scientist develops a hypothesis which is tested through research. Once the research is completed the scientist publishes his or her findings so others can replicate the research.

When marketing is defined as the scientific method

translated into a business setting, physicians seem less threatened about its implications.

What is the difference between a customer and a consumer?

Definitions in Webster's dictionary compare the consumer and customer quite vividly. The customer is someone who *purchases* a commodity or service. The emphasis is on purchasing. The consumer is someone who *uses* an economic good. The emphasis is on utilization.

In the current health care environment the insurance company, health plan or government payor who actually purchases the service on behalf of a patient is the customer. The patient who actually uses the service is the consumer. The physician who directs the purchase of a service on behalf of a patient becomes an intermediary in the process but one with very distinct ties to both the customer and the consumer.

To complicate the issue, Roget's International Thesaurus suggests *buyer* and *purchasing agent* as synonyms for *customer*. Although this is consistent with Webster's definition, Roget's uses *user* and *buyer* as synonyms for *consumer*.

In the section on building trust among managers and the medical staff you suggest the administrator spend time in the physician's lounge. Do you have any suggestions on how the novice administrator can do this?

The concept of managing in the physicians' lounge emphasizes the importance of less structured communication with the medical staff. Interaction in the lounge provides an opportunity for the administrator to get to know the medical staff member on the doctor's own turf.

The administrator who feels comfortable being in the physicians' lounge without a specific agenda—like dropping off the *Wall Street Journal*—should be commended. Dropping off the *Journal* is just that, a reason for the administrator's presence in the physicians' lounge so the administrator feels more comfortable initiating informal conversation. If the administrator does in fact feel a need for an excuse, it should be a natural one and one consistent with the administrator's style.

When you share marketplace data with your medical staff, don't you run the risk of having a psychological, if not physical, bail out if the data present you in a weak position? How do you prevent this?

When sharing any market data with the medical staff, department heads or employees you should plan carefully. Reference to two concepts introduced in this book will help the administrator grappling with the most effective way to share data.

The hour glass philosophy of physician involvement in market planning suggests that at the beginning of a process there is maximum opportunity for involvement by the medical staff. But as the process reaches a strategic decision point, fewer and fewer physicians are involved. Typically, as the strategic decision point is reached, physician participants are coproviders and not competitors. Physicians should have an opportunity for input at the beginning of the process, and their thoughts, along with comparative market share data, should be presented to a well briefed marketing task force. By the time strategic decisions are made and the facility is ready to communicate these to the medical staff again, responses have been developed to reverse the hospital's weak position.

For the uninitiated, bad news is like Castor Oil: it should only be given in small doses. Because physicians' time is frequently limited, the administrative representatives on the marketing task force would probably be in a better position if they presented market share data in a narrow area and gave physicians an opportunity to discuss the implications of this data and appropriate responses all in the same meeting rather than taking one session to present all market data, another session to discuss implications, and a third session to discuss responses.

Why are authors spending so much time today discussing the need to establish relationships between providers and hospitals?

In recent years there have been some fundamental changes in the incentives which drive the health care system. Prospective payment, contracting, an oversupply of physicians and an excess of hospital beds have contributed to these changes. With government paying such a large percentage of the nation's health care bill, it's having a controlling influence on how health care is delivered. In an era of "us" against "them," hospitals and physicians are realizing that if providers and health care facilities can cooperatively be "us" they will be much more successful in addressing "them"—the government, large insurance companies, or dominant payor groups.

Physicians' loyalties are shifting and in many communities groups of physicians and hospitals are becoming more closely aligned for purposes of contracting and delivery of health care. Hospitals and physicians alike are nervous about the implications of these changes and in many cases hesitate to cooperate on *anything*. The successful hospital and physician providers of the future, however, will be those who have maintained flexibility to cooperate when appropriate, plan together so they can control their own destiny, and be clean competitors when this approach is indicated.

Where do the concepts of product line marketing and cost accounting fit into the hospital's overall acceptance of marketing principles?

It would be unrealistic to assume that a hospital without a marketing orientation and with a traditional finance department could move directly to product line marketing supported by an automated cost accounting system. This will be an evolutionary process. Depending on the orientation of the administrative staff, employees and medical staff, the time needed to make these changes will be several months or several years.

Sophisticated computer systems are necessary to support an automated cost accounting program. The hospital may need to make operational and financial decisions several years in advance to support this type of expenditure.

Even if the hospital is in the early stages of realizing that marketing and advertising are not synonymous, and that marketing requires research, planning, communications and evaluation, many of the principles discussed in this book can be applied. Whether the hospital is embarking upon a product line marketing program or a more generic facility-wide marketing effort, physicians should be involved. The methods for classifying physicians and the models for physician research and physician involvement on marketing task forces can be used easily. As we have discussed, the PRIMOe marketing model is flexible enough that it can be used on a department-wide, product line or facility-wide basis. We have even used it with groups of hospital volunteers to assist in developing marketing plans for fund raisers and the hospital's gift shop.

Being behind in the marketing curve is no excuse for not starting at all. It means that the facility should develop a methodical plan to address its marketing needs and bring administrative staff, department heads, employees and the medical staff on board quickly and with little trauma.

Many organizations offer opportunities for administrators, department heads and physician leaders to begin learning about the appropriate applications of marketing principles in the institution. Physician participation in marketing seminars offered by professional organizations can be very valuable. Frequently, these sessions are structured as opportunities for administrators, trustees and physicians to participate jointly in learning about current and future trends. Many department heads probably have had or will be able to attend sessions on marketing in their particular area of expertise at state or national professional society meetings. You should encourage this participation and structure opportunities for these people to share their new knowledge with others when they return to the hospital.

A second step may be to provide structured opportunities for groups of physicians from your own medical staff or your department heads to participate in educational sessions on marketing, product line marketing or physician involvement in marketing. Inviting a guest speaker to address a physician symposium or department head retreat is a good opportunity to lay the ground work for future action.

Acceptance of the marketing process is frequently related to an individual's participation in the planning cycle and ability to use data which emerges. Guest relations programs which are structured as marketing opportunities will be much more successful and can provide a direct day-to-day link with the novice department head. When patient satisfaction research results are shared with physicians, department heads and employees, their buy-in to the need for effective product development, positioning, communications and evaluations will be dramatically heightened.

In discussing the PRIMOe model, you indicate that a mission statement should be developed by facility management before determining which method for physician interaction would be most appropriate. Wouldn't physician commitment be stronger if the doctors were actually involved in setting the direction of the organization?

Ideally, administrative and physician representatives discuss and recommend the direction for the organization. The organization's mission is then established by the facility's board where there is physician involvement.

The marketing mission of a particular product line is an assessment of the financial or community service direction the activity should take. Is the hospital marketing its OB unit to increase the contribution to the bottom line to make a specific amount of money or to offer a comprehensive package for contracting, etc? This initial decision needs to be made before physicians who are patient brokers or competitors become involved in market planning activities. Frequently, physicians unfamiliar with the marketing process hold the belief that the reason for marketing a particular product line is "to deliver a quality service to the community." In the new competitive era in which hospitals find themselves, this is no longer enough. Provision of quality health care services is obviously a goal that should be actualized in objective statements which are part of the marketing plan and evaluated to ensure quality services are being delivered. However, the hospital which has not established a business purpose for marketing a particular product line cannot be guaranteed success in today's environment.

2

REAL WORLD EXAMPLES

This book begins with brief descriptions of five success stories, examples of how hospitals drew physicians into the product line marketing process. This part offers details of those case histories, describing exactly how and in what ways doctors contributed to the development of marketing programs and to their implementation.

Each of these examples is narrated by someone intimately familiar with the experience, a member of the hospital staff who worked in the program.

Geriatrics

Marsha A. Vacca

Physicians were involved in the development of a geriatrics program product line marketing plan through participation on a multidisiplinary task force. This is not a new model for the Sutter Community Hospitals organization; it had been used successfully in other clinical service areas.

Sutter Community Hospitals is the acute care affiliate of Sutter Health System. The system is a diversified, multihospital organization with acute care hospitals, skilled nursing facilities, outpatient surgery centers, and a home IV therapy corporation. Two hundred forty-eight bed Sutter General Hospital, and 378-bed Sutter Memorial Hospital are the flagship hospitals.

The geriatrics multidisciplinary task force was made up of key department managers representing allied services, nursing administration, clinical program directors and identified medical directors. Functional specialists such as discharge planners and social services personnel, hospital administrators, and physicians from a variety of different specialty areas also served on the task force. The task force was established before the development of a marketing plan was considered. When it was initially formed its purpose was to serve as an advisory body to the Director of Geriatric Programs. As such, its stated mission was:

- To provide a communications link between the geriatric program and other hospital departments.
- To assist in an on-going needs assessment for geriatrics program development.
- To review geriatric program strategies and advise on their implementation.
- To work cooperatively on interdepartmental geriatric programs.

Since a multidisciplinary task force already existed, it became apparent that it would be expeditious to involve this group in the development of a product line marketing plan. Since the task force was a very large group, it had traditionally reached consensus by discussing change and augmenting recommendations which were brought before it by staff representatives. For example, although the task force was responsible for developing a mission statement for geriatric programs at Sutter, this philosophical statement of the facility's approach to dealing with older patients and their family members as well as the community at large was initially laid out by staff and then discussed by the task force.

The task force was heavily involved in primary research and analysis of the older market in Sacramento. A community study, physician focus groups, and staff focus groups were conducted. A subcommittee of the original task force—augmented by other key physician representatives—provided direction and input on the marketing survey instrument design and in reviewing and analyzing the results of the research activities.

In retrospect, the research conducted during the development of the marketing plan probably should have been more extensive. Focus groups both before and after the quantitative telephone study would have provided opportunities to assimilate options for discussion by seniors.

Although specific new program components did not directly result from the research, there were many key findings which have guided program development. The research with the medical staff and consumers emphasized the fact that the hospital needed to pay more attention to its family and general practice physicians who were generating a large number of admissions as well as specialty referrals. The research also served as a catalyst for a skilled nursing care facility proposal for the organization. Other direct results of the research are not as esoteric but have had profound effects on day to day patient care. For example, staff members who participated in employee focus groups pointed out the disorientation and confusion many patients experienced because there were no specific objects or symbols to orient them in their room. Since then, clocks have been placed in the patient rooms and sign boards have been added to the decor. The signs serve several purposes. It's an opportunity to write cheerful messages to the patients who they see on a regular basis. The message boards can also be used to communicate with staff members, physicians and families.

The geriatric task force has also been instrumental in designing and developing specific programs and services for older adults and their families, both within the hospital setting and within the community. Such programs as family support, community health education, annual professional geriatric symposia, and the development of a self-care approach to patient care were the results of the task force's activities. The task force has truly been the initiator of a number of different programs and services for older patients and their families at Sutter Community Hospitals.

Some of the strengths of working with physicians through a multidisciplinary task force include:

- The task force has been a key group of managers, administrators and medical staff members who have kept abreast of trends in geriatrics through dissemination of articles and discussions at task force meetings as they have become better educated in what geriatric medicine and geriatric care issues are all about. They have been able to initiate a number of programs and changes in operations for the organization. A prime example of this is the self-care approach to patient care at Sutter General. The proposal which came from the task force was an attempt to re-orient the organization's philosophy of how patients are cared for. Everyone agreed staff needed to "get patients up and walking" as soon as possible.

- By having physicians involved on the task force we were able to draw from many medical staff departments and specialty areas. These included neurology, oncology, family practice and internal medicine. Thus, we were able to make a very clear statement about the complexity of the medical situations that often confront older patients and their families. Many specialists must work closely together in order to provide adequate and appropriate care for the older person.

- By involving both physicians and key ancillary service managers on the task force, we were able to model the concept of a multidisciplinary team approach to geriatric care which is a cornerstone of providing comprehensive geriatric services.

- By having physicians on the task force we were able to obtain immediate and firsthand information on how best to reach one of the major target markets for the geriatric program—the medical staff. This has definitely worked and has been very helpful. Both formal and informal channels are now used for communicating with the medical staff.

- The task force has provided the physician members an opportunity to get to know the resources within the hospital organization. Physician members of the task force talk to their medical staff colleagues and to employees when they feel resources can be used more appropriately. A primary example of this is increased referrals to a hospital based resource known as Lifeline, an emergency response system for elderly patients who are being discharged. Many physicians are now writing orders for this service.

- Because geriatric medicine is still a maturing clinical service, having key members of the medical staff—who have shown an interest in working with older patients and their families and are respected by the rest of the medical staff—on the task force has helped bring credibility to this new service and its program development.

In spite of these many strengths there are some weaknesses inherent in using the multidisciplinary task force approach. These include:

- We had to recognize the need for confidentiality in discussing the hospital's strategic positioning and marketing concerns. It has been difficult having physicians serve on the task force when most doctors at Sutter have privileges at a major competitor's facilities. Because many physicians are patient brokers and not coproviders we have had to be extremely selective about which doctors are chosen to serve on the task force.

- It is hard to identify physicians who can be visionaries or pathfinders as well as clinicians. We needed doctors who could deal in the broader philosophical issues and see how they interfaced with daily patient care needs and concerns. We found that this type of physician was indeed difficult to identify and have, therefore, spent our time educating doctors on how to accept this role.

- It is difficult to find physicians who understand or have an awareness of product line marketing, particularly when, at the same time, many of them are struggling with the whole philosophical approach of whether marketing within the health care field is appropriate. Many physicians are caught between their own thoughts and feelings about marketing and where today's health care environment is pushing the health care field. Doctors are indeed becoming accustomed to marketing. The task force has provided an opportunity to educate doctors on the full spectrum of marketing. They in turn are educating their colleagues.

- If the task force does not meet very frequently or on a regular basis it becomes difficult to build a trusting, supportive relationship among the task force members. This needs to be there. One of the major barriers that we had to overcome was the concept of "us" versus "them". Depending on the participant's perspective, "us" was the private practicing physicians on the hospital medical staff and "them" was the hospital administration. Getting everyone to work together and to create a common perspective so they can work effectively together is, at times, an ongoing struggle. To be most effective, a working task force should meet every six to eight weeks. If the full task force is only going to be minimally involved in market based planning activities, it perhaps could meet quarterly with subcommittees meeting more frequently.

- Often the physician members of the task force and the key department managers and nursing staff members find themselves hesitant to say what they really believe or feel with their peers in the room. Task force members have to learn how to deal effectively with one another as a task force and yet still be able to work with each other on the nursing units on critical patient care matters. The tone set by the task force chair or administrative coordinator is critical to the development of a team concept in which physicians, department managers, and nursing staff members can all participate effectively.

In evaluating what we could have done differently, the development of a medical directorship for geriatrics comes immediately to mind. Obviously, five years ago when Sutter began its geriatrics program development, the field was very much in its infancy. Now there is a clear need to identify a medical director of geriatric services. Ideally, the physician would have training and background in geriatric medicine and have worked in this field since receiving university based training. The doctor must have an ongoing commitment to continuing education and communicate a broad range of philosophy and training needs for health care professionals working in geriatrics.

Finally, the entire geriatric task force could have been used more effectively in developing and analyzing the marketing research. Follow-up targeted qualitative and quantitative consumer marketing research to benefit geriatric program development has not been conducted following the initial marketing plan development. The task force has been using very valid and creditable secondary research which has proved effective, but added strength could have been brought to the geriatric program by updating primary geriatric research on an ongoing basis.

Marsha A. Vacca is Geriatric Program Director at Sutter Community Hospitals, Sacramento, California.

Heart Center

Steven A. Fellows

Product line management and product line marketing have inherent difficulties: Both assume the ability to "lump" patients into a centralized line of service; both consolidate a sophisticated array of clinical services; both tend to carry a negative connotation with the health care professional. Management has been adept at responding to what appears to be whimsical changes in the health care industry. Less adept at change have been licensed hospital personnel including medical technologists, respiratory care practitioners, nurses, physicians and the like. Even more so, physicians see the terminology of "product line" and "marketing" as incongruous to the endeavor of pursuing patient care.

If this is true, then how is any organization or institution supposed to overcome the negative impressions of physicians in product line "anything?" Furthermore, if one's competition has a supportive medical staff who do not hold the same beliefs as your medical staff on product line services and marketing, how do you compete? Will you be able to survive? What if your survival is based upon the key service component of your institution, i.e., cardiology services?

These were the precise questions addressed in 1984 when Sutter Memorial Hospital was in the initial development phase of a new marketing plan for its cardiology services. With a conservative medical staff numbering over 850, one driving force behind the financial viability of the institution is its cardiac care. Nearly 40 percent of gross revenue and 60 percent of return on net equity were attributed to coronary care. The advent of DRGs and indemnity/contract (insurance) providers had a significant effect upon the bottom line of the institution. In addition, the smaller rural hospitals dotting Northern California were suddenly opening catheterization laboratories, hiring cardiologists and even looking into open heart surgical services. Such dramatic changes posed a real threat to the institution.

As background information, Sutter Memorial Hospital is owned and operated by Sutter Health System, a multi-hospital health care system based in Sacramento, California. Sutter Memorial is a 378-bed tertiary referral care center located in a suburban area, east of downtown Sacramento.

Today over 900 adult and pediatric open heart procedures are performed there annually. The medical staff consists of seven full-time cardiovascular surgeons and 62 invasive cardiologists; over 120 beds are dedicated to the care of cardiac patients.

The institution relies on referrals to local physicians,

a practice which appeared to be in jeopardy. Not-for-profit and for-profit firms were all itching to get a piece of the Sutter action. At the same time attempts were being made by local hospitals and their medical staffs to redirect these patients to their facilities. Pediatric cardiology was split between Sutter and the local university medical center. However, neither institution had a "major" share of the market. Members of the medical staff were split on the moral and ethical perspectives of product line services. Marketing was a dirty word. Nursing staff, while not excited about the new direction health care was moving, were nevertheless open to the changes as long as the "quality" of patient care was not undermined.

The groundwork was set in place before a meeting of the members of the heart steering committee. In 1980 an initial meeting of professionals was convened when Sutter initiated its "centers of excellence" program. The heart program was one of several centers designated. These individuals agreed in principle on a center of excellence entitled the "Northern California Heart Institute" but questioned its meaning, significance and appropriateness. Promotional materials were generated, but the Institute kept a fairly low profile until 1984.

Numerous discussions were held with administrative and management personnel to strategize and develop a plan to ensure a successful and productive steering committee. Initially it was thought physicians could be left out of the planning. However, with what we were trying to accomplish—solidifying physician loyalty and commitment to the institution—their involvement was felt to be essential. Fortunately, the local competition had not yet begun any programs of this nature.

As with any institution, there were factions of physician groups who competed with each other. Yet it was our firm belief that in spite of some split loyalties, all major physician groups had to be represented. This was a deliberate attempt to try and sway the loyalties of physicians from the competitors back to more solid support for Sutter.

Preliminary discussions between the Associate Administrator and the Administrative Director of Cardiology Services identified which physicians would be asked to participate in the program, identification of who would conduct the background research, how the steering committee would be established, who would chair the committee, and how to deal with physicians who were diametrically opposed to "product line" services.

From the outset we were convinced physicians had to have an active role in product line development. Why? Because patients by-and-large are referred from one physician to another and to a hospital based upon pre-established relationships. This being the case, it was essential that a broad representation of the medical staff be included on the Steering Committee. After all, the cardiovascular surgeon is at the end of a long line of referrals. Initial secondary research revealed that nearly 35% of all cardiac patients came from communities contiguous with Sacramento. This indicated that a lengthy line of referrals had to occur just for the patient to show up at Sutter Memorial Hospital.

For example, a patient from Auburn (40 miles northeast of Sacramento) would normally see an OB/Gyn or family physician for a complaint of a coronary nature. In turn, this doctor would refer the patient to a general internist in the local community who is better equipped to handle such conditions. Once the internist realized the patient needed greater assistance and more specialization than he or she could provide, the patient was referred to a cardiologist at Sutter Memorial Hospital. After a preliminary diagnostic workup, if catheterization was necessary the patient would be admitted and a heart cath performed. If the patient was a candidate for Percutaneous Transluminal Coronary Angioplasty (PTCA), most likely another cardiologist specializing in angioplasty would be brought in to perform the procedure. However, at the same time the cardiovascular surgeon would be called in to stand by as back-up for the PTCA in the event of complications. Not until the heart cath films were reviewed did the cardiovascular surgeon really get involved. This process could take weeks or a matter of hours depending upon the patient's condition.

Physicians selected to serve on the committee were representative of this medical staff: Cardiovascular surgeons, adult cardiologists, and pediatric cardiologists. Critical care nursing personnel, administrative and operations management were also on the committee. Primary care practitioners were also included since the major/primary source of referrals came from this segment of the medical staff.

Physicians were screened based upon their commitment and loyalty to the organization and their willingness to "openly and actively" participate in a positive manner in all aspects of the committee's charge. This included a strong commitment to attend *all* meetings. Each participant was informed who the other members of the committee would be in an attempt to reinforce the credibility of the committee's purpose. In addition, screening looked at physicians' admitting practices. Contacts for participation were made personally by the Associate Administrator and then follow-up encouragement came from the Administrative Director. This team effort paid off well.

Research was conducted in a two-tiered process. The organization's planning department and information systems group were utilized to provide initial data on patient origins, demographic data and physicians who participated in patient care. This information was then coordinated into a packet for the initial meeting.

The second tier of research involved the preparation of hospital data. A SWOT (strengths, weaknesses, opportunities, and threats) analysis was performed. This ultimately lead to a full-scale research analysis via interviews and multiple focus group sessions.

The steering committee identified referring physicians' groups, physicians as a whole in the Sacramento community and in outlying areas, staff members, community members, patients, etc., to be interviewed in order to verify the SWOT of the Sutter Heart Program, what they liked/didn't like about it, etc. The committee reviewed all questions to be asked, the techniques to be employed in conducting the research, and even submitted recommendations for other physicians to be interviewed.

Eventually, all accumulated research data was consolidated and presented to the Steering Committee for review. Support was also sought for recommendations to improve the overall service.

Even after all the planning and preparation that went into developing the steering committee, there were still physicians who had a very negative attitude toward marketing. Regardless of how you packaged product line development, it was still marketing. The very term seemed to connote a cheapening of the business of caring for sick patients.

Much time and effort initially was spent in education and explaining to physicians not only the changes taking place in the health care industry, but allowing for open communication and interchange to discuss some deep-seated feelings. Management decided we needed to first overcome the misconceptions of marketing and product line development before we could deal with the issues.

In an amazing turnaround, the most difficult physicians, those individuals who took strong exception to the whole area of marketing, suddenly became ardent supporters of product line development. While they supported what was being researched and developed, they nevertheless were still opposed to "promotional or "advertising" materials. Yet the committee proved to be a vibrant force which, in effect, generated positive change for the course of the heart program.

After nearly seven months of meetings, the research was prepared and distributed to members of the Steering Committee. At the subsequent meetings, information was disclosed in great detail. Considerable discussion was generated on all issues, most specifically that dealing with referals.

The impetus to Sutter and the receiving physicians was to assure continued satisfaction in communications with the referring physicians.

Numerous additional recommendations were made involving nursing services and ancillary support services. Most interesting was the Sacramento public's desire for more educational information on heart disease, thereby placing a higher priority on the prevention of coronary disease. In this respect, all members of the Steering Committee agreed that cardiac rehabilitation should be the focal point for advertising, promotion, etc., of hospital services.

Finally, the "Northern California Heart Institute" did not have significant meaning to the public at large or to the medical staff for that matter. There was no association of the Institute with Sutter Memorial Hospital. Since this was the case, the name was changed to the "Sutter Heart Institute" and promoted in a professional and acceptable manner.

Following are some of the action plans which responded to patient care needs:

- All cardiac nursing care units were under remodeling and/or construction when the issues were addressed. Patient recommendations were incorporated. These included private family areas, availability of telephones, a more conducive environment to family waiting including televisions, art work, furnishings, etc., which supported families of patients;

- A new emphasis on guest relations was initiated;
- A change in visitation hours for families of cardiac patients and the acceptance of children, under parental guidance, visiting on the cardiac units;
- Expansion of patient education materials developed and designed specifically for Sutter patients, under guidance of physicians on the Steering Committee;
- Development of a wellness program, inpatient cardiac rehabilitation program, executive fitness program, etc., under the umbrella of cardiac services;
- Rearrangement of management personnel in Cardiology Services to better coordinate product line development;
- Development of outpatient and mobile cardiac diagnostic services and personnel to support patient care;
- A sophisticated and subtle advertising plan to "get the Sutter Heart Institute" story out to the Sacramento community;
- Recruiting of pediatric cardiologists;
- Development of fund raising efforts to support research, continuing education, patient education, and promotional materials in conjunction with Sutter Hospitals Foundation;

- Establishment of a committee structure of physicians, patient care personnel, etc., to provide continued support and direction of the Sutter Heart Institute.

Much can be said about physician involvement in product line marketing. The most important aspect is that physicians are involved from the beginning and not precluded from participation because they may not understand the process or significance behind the need to be able to respond to the competition's encroachment onto your turf. Education is essential as is understanding and a well thought-out plan. A successful operation can only be realized when the whole team actively and energetically participates together. While split loyalties may be cause for concern, participation can also swing physicians back to a more loyal position because they've been involved in the process, whereas before they had been excluded. Today they have an arena in which to be heard and appreciated.

Sutter has successfully implemented nearly all of the recommendations identified in the research. But we still have a long way to go and a constant battle to assure we do not lose sight of our primary purpose, that of providing the highest quality patient care at the lowest cost possible. The Sutter Heart Institute's motto has become, "High Technology, High Touch." I believe we are not only maintaining our current market share but have actually seen an increase due to the commitment and dedication of professional personnel and physicians who guide and direct the Sutter Heart Institute.

Steven A. Fellows is Administrative Director at the Sutter Heart Institute, Sutter Memorial Hospital, Sacramento, California.

Obstetrical Services

Karen Corrigan

Norfolk General Hospital's market based planning efforts began in 1983 with research that resulted in a portfolio analysis of the facility's major clinical programs. Based on this analysis the hospital decided to direct its attention to 16 potential product lines. A team approach was taken to product management. Four teams were assigned the responsibility for developing marketing plans for each of four product lines. Their charge was to initiate or formalize additional research and determine how the product line should be developed.

Norfolk General Hospital is a part of Alliance Health System, a Virginia-based health management organization. It is Alliance's corporate philosophy that decentralized middle management personnel be involved in decision-making processes. This research and philosophy set the stage for looking at Norfolk General's obstetrical program.

At the time market based planning efforts began, the biggest question was whether or not Norfolk General should stay in the delivery of obstetrical services at all. Half of its patients were covered by Medicaid or had no financial resources. The physical facility was old, and although the hospital was the only perinatal center in the region, it did not have a reputation among consumers for its premature nursery care. Additionally, as the primary teaching hospital for the Eastern Virginia Medical School, the major emphasis of the program was on complicated deliveries.

Only one private practice physicians' group augmented the services offered by the medical school's obstetrical teaching program and the hospital was frequently viewed as an obstetrical center merely for complicated pregnancies—not someplace for women who were not expecting any problems. In addition to all of these challenges, the hospital was seeing increased competition from other facilities which were successfully luring private pay patients to other obstetrical programs.

The product management team assigned the responsibility of developing a marketing plan for the OB program conducted consumer and physician research. Part of the physician research was soliciting recommendations on facility changes that were necessary. This input indicated the need for a $3.5 million renovation plan.

The consumer research with women pointed Norfolk General in the direction of the development of a women's health pavilion. Women who participated in the research wanted access to more health education and resources (such as support groups) in addition to improvements in the physical facility. Specific consumer research included focus groups with women in the general public as well as past patients. The hospital also conducted a quantitative telephone survey with women in the service area. Secondary data analysis helped support findings about program components, which women were looking for. Most of the physician research was conducted on an informal basis and was designed to supplement a more formalized broad based physician study, which the facility conducts every two years.

The research was directed by the marketing task force, which included representatives from many areas of the hospital. Task force members were encouraged to talk to OB employees as well as medical staff members to supplement more formalized research being undertaken.

Based on this research, the marketing task force went to the hospital's management and recommended that the facility remain in the obstetrical business, focus on the development of a women's health pavilion, and begin the suggested renovations. A major component supporting the recommendation was the knowledge that members of the medical staff were committed to supporting these marketing efforts and were encouraging the recruitment of additional physicians who could support the new unit. The board agreed with the recommendation and the renovations were scheduled for completion at the end of 1986.

Physician input into the specific design of the new department was structured through the medical staff's formal OB/Gyn committee. Individual and small group presentations of research results provided an opportunity to solicit input into the facility and product design. This was largely conducted on an informal basis.

The medical staff also set up a physicians' educational advisory group that assisted the facility as it implemented a more aggressive health education program. The facility hired a full-time health educator who developed a telephone information service for women as well as additional educational forums on subjects from health to law to finance. Members of the OB/Gyn staff are regular speakers for the health forums.

When the decision was made to implement a women's health marketing plan, a standing marketing task force was developed. The task force members are clinical and management representatives from both the Women's Health Pavilion and other hospital departments. Physicians are used on an ad hoc basis. The group meets monthly to look at operations, develop marketing goals and objectives, and assign projects. The task force has subcommittees which deal with specific functions. For example one subcommittee is responsible for interfacing with the perinatologists, another with the obstetricians.

Even as the facility construction was underway, the hospital added 24-hour OB anesthesia coverage—again based on physician research. Image building and public advertising on the Women's Health Pavilion was conducted. The central message was that consumers had requested this type of service.

The activities helped to change physician opinions. Obstetricians who were borderline admitters have been affected most by the program. Hospital representatives visited their offices and helped develop specific marketing packages for these doctors. Additionally, preferred provider arrangements have been negotiated with several area businesses.

Norfolk General's marketing efforts have produced dramatic results. From an OB census of 2,600 in 1984, the facility had more than 4,000 deliveries in 1986. Much of this increase is the result of the addition of 16 new private practice OB/Gyns to the staff. Perhaps even more dramatically, the payor mix of patients is now 75% private pay instead of the previous 50% Medicaid or no pay.

Norfolk General sees several benefits in involving physicians in the product line marketing process:

- Physicians are in an excellent position to help design the product. They receive input from their patients which can be used directly by the facility in program development.

- Physicians are the actual users of the OB services at the hospital. It's important to remember that advertising *does not* sell a product. It may pique interest or develop an image but it does not directly put patients in the hospital. *Doctors put patients in the hospital.*

In spite of the dramatic successes which Norfolk General has seen, marketing task force representatives are likely to seek additional physician involvement in the future. More formalized involvement of physicians will be necessary as the market place becomes more complicated. This probably is more feasible today, particularly at a facility like Norfolk General. Physicians make time to attend planning and marketing sessions and are more willing to get involved in the process today than they were just a few years ago. Most physicians ask and volunteer to participate.

Although the results have been dramatic, the successes perhaps would be even greater if it had been possible to complete the renovations more quickly so even more new patients could be accommodated.

Karen Corrigan is Director of Marketing Services at Norfolk General Hospital, Norfolk, Virginia.

Oncology Services

Stanley B. Berry

Sonora Community Hospital is a private nonprofit institution owned and operated by a religious health care corporation based in California. The hospital consists of 67 medical/surgical beds, 7 ICU/CCU beds, a 14-bed free-standing birthing center and a 32-bed distinct part skilled nursing facility. First established in the mid-1950s, the hospital serves 40,000 residents living in the "Mother Lode" area of the Central Sierra Foothills of California. The hospital's medical staff is comprised of 60 physicians, 75 per cent of whom are specialists. Most medical problems can be handled by one of two local hospitals. Major head trauma, spinal cord injuries, extensive burns, open heart procedures, and many forms of cancer are referred to larger communities, 50 to 60 miles outside of the hospital service area.

Like other rural hospitals in the West, Sonora Community has seen its census and its inpatient revenue base decline under current prospective payment systems. To preserve the hospital as a major provider of health care in its service area, administration saw a need to develop a strategic and long-range plan for the hospital. As a first step in this process, a quantitative study of health care attitudes of residents was conducted. Three hundred area residents, selected randomly, were contacted by phone and interviewed by trained professionals using a survey questionnaire. The data was then analyzed and submitted to the hospital.

This survey yielded a wealth of information the hospital has subsequently used in its planning process and in the development of a comprehensive marketing plan. Finding out what people want and then delivering the service or product is an age old concept that has made the difference between a successful and an unsuccessful business for millennia. The hospital successfully followed this rule when it launched a very successful hospital based urgent care program after noting that one-third of those interviewed identified the need. Visits to the emergency department have increased 30 percent. Based on this and other successful applications of information derived from the survey, hospital administration decided to expand the survey process to include hospital employees, board members, specific groups in the community, and its own medical staff.

Initially, the survey of the medical staff was limited to the area of oncology. The hospital wanted to know if there was physician support for formalizing oncology services, which were being provided on a piecemeal basis within the community. A general survey which would normally have preceded a more narrow or selective survey was postponed because administration felt an immediate need to begin developing an oncology product line. This decision was based upon community support, a need to improve and expand existing oncology services as suggested by key members of the medical staff, and the opportunity to fill empty beds, diversify revenue, and differentiate the hospital from its competitor.

The physician survey was actually an integral part of a total feasibility study on oncology. The survey process involved face-to-face interviews with selected surgeons, internists and family practice physicians. This group was comprised of both "supporters" and "non-supporters" of the hospital. It was felt that such a divergent group would offer a more balanced opinion and perhaps even garner support for formalized oncology services on the part of "non-support" physicians, since it would be available to serve all patients. It should be noted that no physicians in the area limited their practice to only one of the two competing hospitals.

Although the interview process itself was kept brief, the interviewers found it difficult to set up appointments with some physicians, especially those who were very busy and protective of their time, or felt the hospital had some ulterior motive in mind. Some interviews were conducted on a group basis following regular meetings of medical staff departments. These had only limited success since interviews were often held after the meeting's agenda had been covered and physicians were anxious to leave while others simply left. By far, the most valuable input came from one-on-one interviews within the physician's office. While it took longer than anticipated to complete all of the interviews, all targeted physicians were eventually interviewed.

Overall, most physicians were pleased that their input was being sought by the hospital. Although some complained about administration using up their valuable time, even the busier physicians and the "non-support" physicians provided extremely valuable input and often gave the interviewer more time than they had originally intended to.

The results of the interviews indicated strong support for formalizing the hospital's oncology services. It was determined that each physician was referring between one to five patients each week outside of the area for radiation therapy or medical oncology services. All indicated a willingness to use a local oncologist rather than continue referring outside of the area. Physicians even offered specific input as to the ideal traits of an oncologist for the area. Other important comments included the need to strengthen local support services such as hospice care and a clear desire to have the hospital use a particular regional university medical center for patient referral and consultative services. Although physicians felt they were well informed about current cancer therapy, the interviewer, who had considerable expertise in this area, perceived that medical oncology represented the "final effort" in management of patients by the medical staff. Her final report pointed out that physician education may indeed improve the image of medical oncology and result in even a greater number of referrals.

Based primarily on the information obtained from physician interviews, the decision was made to take immediate steps to formalize oncology services at the hospital. These steps included the hiring of a clinical nurse specialist in oncology and the initiation of a referral agreement with the university medical center preferred by the medical staff. Furthermore, a professional physician search firm was hired to recruit an oncologist. The hospital's recruitment efforts were further bolstered when the part-time oncologist serving the area indicated a willingness to form an association with a new oncologist, or at a minimum, share call coverage. Thus far two prospective oncologists have visited and were both very well received by area physicians. Furthermore, both prospective oncologists appreciated the fact that there was strong physician and statistical support for recruiting an oncologist, as evidenced by the final oncology report. Other steps toward formalizing oncology services have included the formation of a tumor board by the hospital and the establishment of a free transportation service to a radiation oncology center in a nearby urban area. The owner of the center—a radiation therapist—is studying with the hospital the feasibility of establishing a satellite unit on the hospital grounds.

Successful administrators create numerous opportunities for physicians to provide feedback and input on hospital plans. Luncheon meetings and hallway consultations with medical staff are important ways to communicate, but communications should not be solely limited to those interactions. A written survey or, in particular, a professionally done interview, may provide the best method for soliciting physician feedback. In this case, several physicians were clearly impressed that the hospital would pay someone to specifically solicit, within their office, comments about the hospital's plans. And these comments came from physicians with whom administration felt they had an open line of communications.

Whether it be because of the formality of the interview process or the promise of anonymity, the information that is gathered and how it is subsequently used is what really counts. In Sonora Community Hospital's case, administration was able to use this information to not only substantiate the need for formal oncology services, but also to gain physician support for following through on this process. When a new oncologist locates in the area, the doctor will be seen as an important resource within the medical community rather than as an unwelcomed competitor or super specialist forced upon the community by the hospital.

The hospital is now conducting a general survey of its medical staff using a written survey form. The hospital has hired an individual to be a professional liaison between the medical staff and the hospital's departments. Besides soliciting physician participation on the various HMO and PPO contracts held by the hospital, she is helping facilitate problem solving between the physician, the office staff, and hospital staff. The hospital president and members of the administrative team continue to play a major role both in keeping the medical staff informed of hospital plans and soliciting new ideas and feedback. After the success experienced with the oncology study, formalized interviews will continue to be a very important method for obtaining physician feedback and support.

Stanley B. Berry is President of Sonora Community Hospital, Sonora, California.

Trauma Care

Peter M. Dawson

Trauma care was one of the first product lines selected for marketing plan development at Norfolk General Hospital. This service was selected because it met several criteria:

- Norfolk General was not well represented in the marketplace for trauma care. Although all acute care facilities had emergency departments, no one had yet moved into provision of trauma care.

- The trauma center complemented other product lines and programs which Norfolk General had. These included neuroscience, a burn center, and a large residency program.

- Trauma care was an emerging product line. Therefore Norfolk General saw a distinctive opportunity to be the first in the marketplace to enter this field.

The provision of trauma services at Norfolk General began in 1981. That year Dr. Bill Schwaab was recruited to start a trauma program at the facility. He headed up a group of medical school surgeons and internists who staffed the trauma team at Norfolk General. Norfolk General is the major teaching hospital of the Eastern Virginia Medical School. Regular emergency department care is provided by a private group of physicians who operate separately from the traumatologist.

A trauma marketing task force was established with Dr. Schwaab at its head. The trauma center then recruited a nurse coordinator. The marketing task force members included physicians, nurses, and administrators. Their initial charge was to develop the systems necessary to implement a trauma program for Norfolk General. Physicians and nurses participating on the task force came from both the medical school and private practice and represented the interests in the emergency department, operating rooms, burn center, and intensive care units. The trauma work group was charged with developing a trauma team that could respond to the community's emergency needs in an organized fashion. Although an assistant administrator was on the committee, most of the staff support was provided by nursing representatives.

The goal of the marketing task force was to ensure that Norfolk General was the first in the area to achieve Level 1 trauma designation. On its way to achieving this goal, the task force met once or twice each month; depending on particular issues which were being developed. Their discussions focused on decision making and idea building. Actual implementation of their recommendations was handled by a variety of subcommittees. For example, in the discussion phases of the marketing task force, slow turn around time in the laboratory was identified as a problem. This issue was delegated to a special lab task force, which was able to solve the problem. At another time, neurosurgical coverage was identified as an issue. Resolution of this problem was assigned to the appropriate physician.

In conducting research necessary to support the development of the marketing plan, the task force spent a considerable amount of time developing systems for response, backup, and support services. Much of their energy was devoted to projecting the impact of a trauma center on the remainder of the hospital. The task force realized that once a trauma patient had been stabilized in the emergency department, the treating physician needed to be concerned about the availability of acute care beds and the resources that would be needed to support the patient during surgery, recuperation and convalescence. Considerable attention was focused on the knowledge that a trauma center was not just a front-in system to get patients into the emergency department but a hospital-wide opportunity to address the ongoing needs of trauma patients. In spite of the recognition of the need for a hospital-wide trauma response system, considerable attention was also devoted to insuring that the appropriate resources were indeed available when these patients were brought into the emergency department.

The Norfolk General trauma center has a number of key components that resulted from the market planning process:

- The 40,000 emergency patients who visit the facility each year are seen by a general emergency speciality group which is separate from the trauma team. The traumatologists have a rotating system of call to insure appropriate coverage throughout the year. They respond to a "trauma alert" by assembling the trauma team within three to five minutes.

- Norfolk General's Burn Trauma Center is supported by an air ambulance system, the only one in the region.

- The hospital has seven different intensive care units, which represent a variety of levels of intensity.

- Following the acute phases for a trauma patient, the hospital has a stroke and spinal cord injury rehabilitation program available for those who need it.

- A community education program is a major component of Norfolk General's trauma center. There are three primary audiences for education: Public safety and health professionals, businesses, and the general public. Part of the education program was designed to "sell" Norfolk General's trauma program to public safety personnel who frequently make the decisions about where patients will go. A specific system has been developed to insure that fire fighters, police, and paramedics receive ongoing feedback to tell them how patients they have brought to the trauma center are progressing. The hospital also provides ongoing continuing education in the trauma area for these public safety officials.

- Norfolk General annually sponsors a regional symposium on trauma. The symposium's target audiences are physicians, nurses, and administrators.

- The industrial audience is another important one for trauma and emergency education. With Norfolk's large ship building and shipping industry, industrial accidents are a frequent source of trauma patients.

- The public portion of Norfolk General's educational campaign focuses on the major causes of accidents and highlights prevention. Slogans such as "drive us out of business, drive 55" and "have a few good belts" (referring to seat belts) help Norfolk General highlight the severity of injuries caused by automobile accidents. Norfolk General also has taken an aggressive posture in explaining to the general public the difference between a trauma center and a more routine emergency department.

Today, 15 to 20 percent of Norfolk General's trauma cases are the result of industrial accidents, primarily from the large ship building and shipping industry. Another 15 to 20 percent of the emergency patients at the facility are victims of knife and gunshot wounds. Ten percent of the patients have been injured in home accidents and the remainder are automobile accident victims.

Today Norfolk General is seeing 1,000 to 1,100 trauma patients each year. Prior to the development of a formalized trauma program and the initiation of the marketing task force, the volume was in the range of 200 to 300 trauma patients each year. These patients are coming from a much broader region. Again, transportation throughout this region is supported by the hospital's air ambulance service, Nightingale.

Having physicians involved throughout the entire market planning process has definitely been a plus for the trauma center. Perhaps four main benefits have emerged:

- The marketing task force and the research the group conducted gave a large number of physicians an opportunity to share their views about emergency and trauma care and how they felt Norfolk General could best respond to the needs of the community.

- Physicians played a major role in identifying issues integral to the success of the trauma center.

- The marketing task force system provided an opportunity to gain early consensus among members of the medical staff regarding the need for a trauma center and the direction its development should take.

- Perhaps most importantly the involvement of physicians has insured that they are the trauma center's key sales people.

At Norfolk General Hospital we know that market based planning needs to focus on the *life* of a project, not merely on the project itself. Therefore an important part of any marketing plan is monitoring and measuring its success over time. Norfolk General had developed a trauma registry which has been designed to monitor the survivability of specific kinds of patients following medical intervention. Ongoing consumer attitude surveys and research with public safety professionals is designed to measure the awareness of the trauma system. Every time a trauma patient comes to Norfolk General it is viewed as an opportunity to test the existing systems and determine how they can be improved and more finely tuned for the future.

It is part of the personality of the Norfolk General organization that the right people should be involved in market based planning. That is why physician involvement in the development of the trauma center was vital. Norfolk General is an organization believing strongly that better products evolve when people who will be involved in their implementation are asked what they want and expect.

Peter M. Dawson is President of First Step, Norfolk, Virginia.

INDEX

A

Administration
  focus groups, 78
  and mission statement, 29–30
  by physicians, 14–15
  and research, 35
  roles of, 19, 21–22
  and trust, 51, 53, 59–61, 82–83
Admitting
  and questionnaires, 66
  tracking, 52
Advertising, 11–12, 22, 25, 27
  evaluation of, 51
  ineffective, 45, 113
  opposition to, 105
  and research, 69–70
  targeted, 46, 47
Alliance Health System, 109
American Cancer Society, 37
American Heart Association, 33
  as competitor, 37

Analysis
  discussed, 31–39
  PRIMOe, 27
  of questionnaires, 66–68
  SWOT, 21–23, 104
  by task force, 98

B

Berry, Stanley B., 115, 120
Budgets, 26
Burn care, 3, 121–122

C

Cancer
  See Oncology
Capitation, 53
Cardiology
  competition in, 52,
  positioning, 43, 45
  purpose, 29, 100–107

research, 36, 71
segmented, 33
share in, 2, 5, 13, 15
task force, 23–24, 58
Catheterization laboratory, 18, 33
competitor, 38
joint venture, 58
Census Bureau, 38
Communication
building, 9
models of, 10–12
Community
and cancer support groups, 32
promotional activities, 54
service products, 28
Competitor, 18, 120
analysis, 37–38
identifying, 47, 52
and joint ventures, 76
and pricing, 78–79
segmentation of, 31–32
Consultants
research, 35
and trust, 59
Consumer
defined, 5, 82
-driven marketing, 45, 63, 69–70
focus groups, 78
identifying, 14, 71, 82
segmentation, 31
Contracting, 53, 84
and pricing, 78–79
Coproviders, 18–19
segmentation of, 32–33, 52
Cost accounting, 54, 85–86

D

Dawson, Peter M., 121, 127
Diabetes, 81
Dichter, Dr. Ernest, 40

Discharge
of geriatrics, 95
DRGs, 100

E

Education
evaluation of, 51
in geriatrics, 94
marketing, 20, 22, 25, 27, 81–82
patient, 16–17, 45
for physicians, 96
prevention, 32, 54, 105–106
and research, 72
safety, 124
women's, 37–38, 110
Employee
focus group, 78
impact on success, 32, 50, 87
research, 36
as salesforce, 39–42
support, 21, 26
Equipment
evaluation of, 51
Evaluation, 51–53
methods, 53–54, 69
of satisfaction, 71
See also Research

F

Feedback, 53, 59, 72, 119
See also Evaluation
Fellows, Steven A., 99, 107
Financing, 50–51
See also Resources
Focus groups
and evaluation, 52
for geriatric programs, 93
multidisciplinary, 34
and research, 22–23, 33, 67–68

size and duration, 78
Fund raising
  See Resources

G

Geriatrics, 2, 5
  and increased market, 59
  marketing plan, 91–98
  organization, 16–17
Goals
  and fiduciary relationships, 77
  and mission statement, 30

H

Heart
  See Cardiology
HMOs, 31, 44, 78, 120
Hospice Care, 118

I

Imaging Centers, 18
Independent contractors
  See Patient brokers
Institute of Motivational
  Research, 40
Insurers, 84
  as consumers, 5, 82
  and health plans, 78
Interviews, 23, 117
  and evaluations, 51
  one-on-one, 30, 34

J

Joint Commission on
  Accreditation
  of Hospitals, 73
Joint ventures, 43, 44, 77
  of catheterization laboratories, 58
  with competitors, 76
  in radiation therapy, 119

L

Lamaze classes, 37
Lavenson, James, 39–42

M

Marketing
  components, 11
  and institutional politics, 19–20
  knowledge of, 22, 81–82
  to preserve market share, 15
  PRIMOe, 27
  product line defined, 5
  See also Mission Statement
Media
  promotions, 46–47
  as target market, 31
Mission Statement
  for geriatric programs, 92
  marketing, 27–30, 87–88
Murray, Bill, 77

N

Needs
  identifying, 26–27
Neurological disease, 5
Norfolk General Hospital, 1, 3, 109, 121
Northern California Heart
  Institute, 101, 105
Nursing staff, 27
  evaluation of, 64
  impact on success, 32

O

Objectives, 47

of patient research, 64
setting, 50–51, 88
Obstetrics/Gynecology, 5
marketing purpose, 29, 80–81
organization, 16–17, 110–113
positioning, 42–43, 45
research, 36–37, 50, 58, 65, 69
segmented, 32
Oncology services, 3, 5
marketing purpose, 29
organization, 16–17, 116–120
positioning, 43, 45
research, 37–38
segmented, 32–33
Ophthalmologists
as competitors, 18
and diabetes, 81

P

Patient brokers, 18–19, 52
Pediatrics, 5
cardiology, 29
Peters, Tom, 38
Physicians
as administrators, 14–15
advisory groups, 12, 14, 80–81
as consumers, 5, 18–19, 31–32, 71
and research, 67
and trust, 51, 53, 58–61, 82–83
Plaza Hotel, NY, 39–42
Politics
institutional, 19–20
Positioning, 30, 42
confidentiality, 96
and research, 87
Positioning: The Battle for Your Mind, 30
PPOs, 31, 44, 78, 84, 120
Pricing, 44–45
and competition, 78–79
PRIMOe model, 27, 85–88

PROs, 38
Product line marketing
defined, 5
Public Relations
community, 2
and patient satisfaction, 64
promotional, 46–47

Q

Quality
assessment, 64–66
strategy, 30
Questionnaires
See Research

R

Recruitment, 58
of female obstetricians, 69, 111
of pediatric cardiologists, 106
search firms, 118
Referrals
evaluation of, 51, 54, 65
to identify involvement, 15–16
and research, 69, 71, 102
segmentation of, 31
and task force, 80
Regulatory approvals, 50
Research, 1, 11, 26
discussed, 31–39
evaluation of, 51, 53–54
for geriatrics program, 93–94
methodologies, 34–36, 67–68
physician involvement in, 21–23, 71
and pricing, 44
surveys, 2–3, 33, 64–66, 72, 120, 126
and trust, 59
Resources
focusing 5, 53

in geriatrics, 95
raising, 17, 37, 50, 86

S

St. Vincent's Hospital (Billings, Montana), 77
Schwaab, Dr. Bill, 122
Segmentation
  of target markets, 31–32
Service
  changes in, 1
  packages, 5, 16
Sharp Memorial Hospital (San Diego), 17
Sonora Community Hospital, 2, 115
Specialists
  Ob/Gyn, 29
  and research, 71
  segmentation of, 31
  in task force, 16
Strategy
  positioning, 42
  quality, 30
Surgeons
  cardiovascular, 24, 43
  as competitors, 18, 52
  Ob/Gyn, 29, 43
  and research, 67

Sutter Health Systems, 2, 91, 100

T

Task force, 2
  chairpersons, 77–78
  choosing, 18–21, 80–81
  establishing, 10, 13
  geriatrics, 91–98
  models of, 14–17
  and target marketing, 33
  trauma marketing, 3
Tracking
  See Evaluation
Trauma care, 3, 121–127
Trust, 10–11, 51, 53
  and involvement, 58, 61, 82–83
  and meeting frequency, 97

V

Vacca, Marsha A., 91, 98
Volunteers
  using PRIMOe, 27, 85–86
  and questionnaires, 65–66

W

Wall Street Journal, 83
Wellness program, 106